Escape to Zion

Volume III in the Emma Trilogy

Escape to Zion

Volume III in the Emma Trilogy

by

Chad G. Daybell

ISBN: 1-55517-501-5
v.1

Published by Bonneville Books

Distributed by:
925 North Main, Springville, UT 84663 • 801/489-4084

CFI Publishing and Distribution Since 1986

Cedar Fort, Incorporated
CFI Distribution • CFI Books • Council Press • Bonneville Books

Typeset by Virginia Reeder
Cover design by Adam Ford
Cover design © 2000 by Lyle Mortimer
Cover model: Rebecca D. Schanderl

Printed in the United States of America

Dedication

To my children,
who will likely live to see
many of these events
actually take place.

Author's Introduction

If you're reading this page, you've likely read *An Errand for Emma* and *Doug's Dilemma,* the first two installments of the Emma Trilogy. I hope you enjoyed them.

By way of explanation, the Dalton family is based on my own Daybell ancestors. Finity, George, Keith and the others were all real people whose lives closely paralleled the experiences described in the novels. Their interactions with Emma and Doug obviously are fictional, but even in those cases, the situations are based on historical events.

This third volume, however, takes the Daltons into the future. So rather than relying on historical family documents for a plotline, I've turned to the words of the Lord's prophets to create a scenario where the Daltons experience many of the final events leading to the Second Coming.

Although I have used the teachings of every latter-day prophet from Joseph Smith to Gordon B. Hinckley in creating this novel, I returned time and again to the words of Joseph F. Smith and his son Joseph Fielding Smith. I'm grateful for the prophetic insight those two men provided about the gospel plan.

Gerald Lund's *The Coming of the Lord* was also an invaluable source as I pieced together the storyline. That book is a compilation of prophecies from the scriptures and the words of latter-day church leaders. I highly recommend it to anyone who wants to learn more about the signs of the times.

The various works of Duane Crowther were also very helpful, especially the books *Prophecy—Key to the Future* and *Inspired Prophetic Warnings*. His uplifting book *Life Everlasting* was also a great source on what awaits us beyond mortality and after the Second Coming.

The intent of this novel isn't to cover every event that will take place between now and the Millennium. Just as *Doug's Dilemma* will never be considered a detailed history of World War II, *Escape to Zion* is just a glimpse through the eyes of a young woman at some of the glorious events that await followers of the Savior. Hopefully many of us will get to take part in some of these events.

I have avoided mentioning specific dates within the novel, but for the sake of the story the reader will sense that Emma has journeyed about three decades into the future. This timeframe was based more on coordinating the ages of the characters in the story rather than an attempt to pinpoint the time of the Second Coming. Besides, if someone reads a copy of this novel 10 years from now, the reader will still feel the story is taking place 30 years in the future. In other words, don't place too much emphasis on the actual timeline.

I thank my extended family for not objecting to this fictional portrayal of our family history. I also thank my immediate family, in-laws and close friends for their encouragement and support from the beginning when *An Errand for Emma* was just a haphazard rough draft entitled *Tripping Through Time*. I also thank these same people for allowing me to send their fictional alter-egos through some crazy situations.

Most of all, I thank my wife, Tammy, for all her love and assistance. She has helped shape these stories more than anyone will ever know.

I hope you like this final installment of the trilogy.

Sincerely,

Chad G. Daybell

Chapter One

"Oh no! Emma, watch out..."
Screech! Bam!

I stared at my shaking, scratched hands as the sound of a collision echoed in my ears. I noticed glass fragments sticking to my sweater, and I carefully touched a throbbing bump on the top of my head.

Then I felt the rumbling.

"Get out of the way," a shirtless man shouted at me. "You'll wreck them!"

I sat up as a large, green-haired woman with pierced lips reached me. She roughly grabbed my elbow and yanked me to the side of the street as two chariots rushed past us. My eyes widened in surprise.

Chariots? The woman let go of me and started dancing wildly. "Yes! Flint won! We'll be partying all night long!" She glanced down at me. "Hey, stay out of the street next time."

"I'm sorry," I mumbled. "I don't know what's going on."

The woman peered at me closely. "Did somebody beat you up? What's your name?"

"Oh, I'm Emma," I said. "Where's my husband? And our car?" I vaguely remembered driving with my husband Tad through downtown Salt Lake on our way to the airport to see my brother Doug return from his mission.

The woman frowned. "You're married? How old-fashioned!" I detected a hint of pity in her eyes as she said, "Well, come join our party if you don't find your husband."

She turned and jogged down the street to where the chariots had stopped. What a strange woman! She seemed too old for that punk-rock look. I gazed around and realized I was sitting in front of the Delta Center, the home of the Utah Jazz.

Or was it? I squinted to read the name on the wall. The Conquest Center? How did I miss that change? A slightly rusted sign attached to the top of the marquee read:

**Salt Lake Gladiatorzz vs.
Las Vegas Lounge Lizards
The battle begins tonight at 7 p.m.
Brought to you by Conquest —
Making your fantasies come true.**

I didn't follow sports too closely, but I'd never heard of the Salt Lake Gladiatorzz. An indoor football team, maybe? Everything seemed completely out of whack. I glanced down the street to see my green-haired rescuer mingling with a slovenly group. They made me nervous, and I crawled across a large plaza in front of the building and rested against a large concrete flower box.

I again heard the pounding of hooves, and another pair of chariots streaked by. I smiled as I got a better chance to examine them. Each chariot was actually the back of a small car that had been sawed in half, with the chariot driver standing in what had been the car's trunk. These were the first chariots I'd ever seen with rubber tires.

Seeing the tires caused me to think again of Tad and our car. I brushed away the last pieces of glass still attached to my sweater, and then everything came rushing back.

"No! This can't be happening," I whispered. "Not another errand!"

I could now clearly recall picking up Tad at his Salt Lake accounting office, where he had taken over the driving duties from me. We had headed to the airport to greet Doug, but then came the collision in the intersection. Tad had shouted out a warning, but it couldn't save me. I had smashed through the car's side window, and the next thing I could recall was my green-haired friend dragging me to safety.

I took another look at my surroundings. I'd never seen Salt Lake in such an ugly condition. Weeds and garbage were everywhere, and the streets were filled with deep potholes. The entire sky was a hazy gray, and the citizens were downright scary. Unfortunately, my clean appearance stood out, and several people were staring curiously at me.

After another pair of chariots passed by, a scruffy middle-aged man in a threadbare tanktop and cut-off Levi's pointed me out to his friends. I quickly looked the other way, but in a moment the man and two bikini-clad women stood before me. They

2

would've been attractive girls, except for the bizarre, colorful tattoos that covered their bodies.

"Those are some fancy clothes you've got," the man said to me. "Where'd you get them? Did you steal them from the Mormons?"

I looked down at my denim jeans, red sweater and bargain-brand tennis shoes. "These aren't anything special," I said nervously.

"Won't you be needing some winter clothing, Tina?" the man asked mischievously. One of the women nodded eagerly, and the man quickly pulled out a knife and pressed it against my neck. "Get to your feet and remove everything," he said smoothly. "I'd hate to slit your throat."

"These clothes are staying right where they are," I said, but not daring to move a muscle.

"We'll see about that," he said. The women grabbed my arms and pulled me to my feet as the man dropped his knife and wrapped one arm around my knees. He used his other hand to begin removing my pants. I screamed and tried to kick the man away. "Help me, somebody!"

A few people turned around to see what was going on, but they turned back to the street as two more chariots headed in our direction. My kicking had hindered the man's progress, but he'd somehow unlatched the top button of my jeans. Meanwhile, one of the women had somehow taken off my watch.

Screech!

The man's hand stopped as he tried to identify the sound. A horse whinnied in pain, and the crowd gasped as a chariot—minus horse and driver—careened off the road onto the plaza.

The chariot sped across the plaza on one wheel, hit the flower pot where I'd been sitting, then it ricocheted right at us. The man and I leaped away, but the poor bikini babes had been frozen in surprise. The chariot hit them at chest-level and scraped loudly to a stop, with the legs of one bikini babe sticking out beneath it. The other woman was now a bloody, tattooed mess a few feet away. The man stared in horror at his fallen females, and I seized the chance to melt into the crowd that was gathering to gawk at the mayhem.

I reached 300 West again and queasily glanced back at the carnage. I didn't see how I could help, and I felt prompted to immediately leave the area. I rebuttoned my jeans and started walking east. The whole city carried an aura of gloom, and I had little hope of finding a safe place. Then a golden glint caught my eye—the statue of Angel Moroni still stood atop the Salt Lake Temple three blocks away. My heart suddenly felt lighter in hopes of finding someone there who didn't look like the star of a freak show.

I cautiously hurried along South Temple, receiving lustful looks and lewd comments from men along the sidewalk. There was no sign of electric power as candles flickered in windows and people gathered around campfires built on the street corners.

I passed a parking lot filled with rusted or stripped cars. In fact, I had yet to see an operating motorized vehicle. A graffiti-covered light-rail station stood in the middle of South Temple—its only occupants were dozens of pigeons. The train rails were rusted and even grown over in spots.

Everything pointed to the fact I'd somehow been bumped into the future—but not too far. Very few new buildings had been added to the skyline. The tallest buildings were badly damaged, with shattered windows and crumbling walls. It depressed me to see how far civilization had slipped. I'd always imagined a future of flying cars and wonderful high-tech gadgets, but Salt Lake was now little more than a ghetto filled with unpleasant people. I couldn't understand it. Where were all the Latter-day Saints?

Chapter Two

I approached Temple Square and found it still surrounded by its imposing concrete wall. It was also encircled by a 10-foot-high chainlink fence. A sign read, "Danger! High voltage. This Fence Is Energized." Thick strands of wire had been placed horizontally on the fence at two-foot intervals, including a strand along the top. So anyone who climbed the fence would certainly have a shocking experience.

The high level of security didn't surprise me, considering the type of people I'd just dealt with. I was baffled at how to get in, though. I noticed the energized fence, angling from the southwest corner of Temple Square also enclosed the Family History Center, the Church History Museum, and seemed to encircle the Conference Center to the north. I didn't see any entrances in the fence, so I continued east until I stood outside Temple Square's southern gate. A sign outside Crossroads Mall across the street caught my eye. It showed McDonalds' golden arches and read, "Come downstairs. We're still open! Try a juicy Big Mac today!" I cringed, trying not to imagine what could be in their Big Mac's Special Sauce.

An older, white-haired man was sitting in a small security booth just inside the gate. He was facing away from me, watching a surveillance monitor. I tried to get his attention by shaking the fence.

Zing! Zing! Zing!

Electricity shot through my arms and I fell backwards. "Yeow! Oh, that hurt," I cried. As I rubbed the tingles out of my arms, I noticed I'd gotten the man's attention. He came to the gate and peered out at me. "How're you feeling?" he asked.

"I'll be all right. I forgot about the electricity."

"Well, don't try to climb the fence," he said. "That top wire will straighten every hair on your body."

The man turned away, but I called after him. "Sir, could you help me? I need to get in there with you."

The man eyed me warily. "If you haven't noticed, Temple

Square is closed to the public."

"I'm LDS. I don't belong out here," I said anxiously.

"Where's the rest of your family?" he asked.

"I don't know," I said. "I can't handle it out here, though. I was attacked."

He looked me up and down. "Well, you look harmless, but last month we let a sweet little girl in here who claimed to be LDS. When she got through the gate she threw two homemade bombs at the temple. The bombs didn't do much damage, but you get the picture."

Another older man appeared at the gate and gave me a suspicious look. "Is everything all right, Brother Nielsen?"

"Oh, hello, Brother Fowers. I'm just talking with this young lady."

Brother Fowers again glanced at me, then his head snapped forward. "What's your last name?" he asked.

"North. Why?"

"I would've sworn you're a Dalton," he said.

Well, Dalton's my maiden name."

"I knew it!" he said with a pleased smile. "You Daltons all look the same."

I was puzzled for a moment, then I imagined Brother Fowers' face 30 years younger and cried, "Aren't you Don Fowers, my brother's friend?"

He gave me a confused look. "I'm Don Fowers, but I doubt I know your brother. Have we met before?"

"Nearly every day, many years ago."

Don squinted his eyes in thought, then recognition came as he whispered, "Emma! I nearly forgot! You're finally here!"

• • • •

Don persuaded Brother Nielsen to let me into Temple Square, but it would be tricky getting me inside. The original Temple Square gate had a padlock, and the gate in the chainlink was also latched. Plus, the electrical wires had to be temporarily turned off.

"We need to do this quickly, or they'll get in," Don said, motioning with his head toward a crowd of unkempt men that were standing near the McDonald's sign. "When I turn off the electricity, unlatch the gate and hurry in."

Brother Nielsen unlocked the black gate, and several scruffy young men sauntered across the street toward us—like hyenas waiting to strike. I watched Don flip a switch in the booth, then I unlatched the gate and slipped between two strands of wire. Most of the men ran to the fence and tried to climb it, but two started to follow me through the gate!

Don restored the voltage the moment I was clear of the wires, and the resulting power surge jolted the heck out of my two pursuers, who'd just straddled the electrified strands. They leaped back and writhed on the ground in agony, while the men who'd climbed the fence were thrown violently to the sidewalk by the surge.

All except one man. He had long, white hair and clung to the fence's top wire with both hands. He let out a loud, crazed laugh as electricity surged through his body. I stared in amazement as his hair shot straight out in all directions. He finally released his grip and dropped to the ground. Our eyes met, and his empty, dead stare made me shiver. I was glad when he calmly walked back across the street.

"Now you see why we're reluctant to turn the power off," Brother Nielsen said as he quickly relocked both gates. "I swear those guys are possessed by demons, just waiting to somehow get in here and tear the place up. Especially that last guy. He's almost inhuman."

"I'm sure his brain is cooked," I said, trying to breathe calmly. "How do you guys ever leave here with all these vultures around?"

Don shook his head. "We don't go anywhere. This is our mission call," he said. "We protect Temple Square. Brigham Young once declared this temple was built to stand through the Millennium, and I'm sure it will—if we can keep it intact until the Second Coming. Thank goodness the brethren were inspired to build a small power station several years ago in the underground parking plaza east of the temple. As you may have noticed, the rest of the city is without electricity."

Don made a sweeping motion with his arms. "This electric fence runs around Temple Square and encompasses the blocks directly north, east and west to protect the church's historical buildings and artifacts," he said. "We hated putting up the fence, but after a few cases of major vandalism, we saw no other option."

"I've seen plenty of scary people in just a few minutes," I said. "I'm not surprised they've tried to destroy such a beautiful place."

"I'm just glad you made it here safely," Don said. "I'm sure you're hungry. Let's get you something to eat."

I thanked Brother Nielsen for his help, then I followed Don into Temple Square's southeast visitors' center. When we were out of earshot, Don put his arm around my shoulder and said, "Your brother Doug told me long ago you'd reappear in my life. He didn't give me any idea when it would be, though."

"You knew I was coming?"

"Sort of," he said. "Right after our missions Doug told me about your adventure in 1868, and then he shared with me his stint with your great-grandpa in World War II. He then explained you'd then been sent on another errand, likely in the future. It sounded unbelievable to me, but I'd never known either of you to be dishonest. Besides, you were missing once again, so the story sounded plausible."

"Yes, these time-traveling errands are the real deal," I said. "But how did you know you'd see me now?"

"After my mission I got married and headed to college in Minnesota, but at our five-year high school reunion Doug took me aside and said, 'Remember those time-travel errands Emma and I went on? Well, she'll need your help someday, so watch for her.' I was stunned by what he'd told me, and I wondered if he was joking, especially when he said, 'All I know is she'll turn up when a metal sign in front of the Delta Center says, "Salt Lake Gladiatorzz vs. Las Vegas Lounge Lizards."'

I nodded enthusiastically. "Yes, that's what it says today!"

Don chuckled at my enthusiasm, then asked, "Do you know how long that sign has been hanging there?"

I shrugged. "A couple of months?"

"Fourteen years," he said tiredly. "That's what the sign said long before I arrived here. Pro sports teams, along with the Utah Jazz, ceased to exist once World War III started. But after the war the guys who had operated professional wrestling filled the void by creating a brutal game called 'Conquest,' an actual battle using swords and spears. It was essentially legalized murder."

I shook my head. "People would pay to watch that stuff?"

"It was a huge success," Don said. "The TV ratings were astronomical."

"How would someone win?" I asked. "By being the last survivor?"

"That's pretty close. There were teams of warriors who would chase each other through a large maze. The spectators would sit in the arena's upper bowl so they could clearly see each of the killings."

This sounded incredibly barbaric. "Did women play too?"

Don nodded. "Each team started with nine men and six women. The team with the most members still breathing on their own after 30 minutes won. Also, fans could buy bags of steel marbles to throw at the warriors, but that naturally always led to fans pelting each other in the stands. Apparently, those fights were more entertaining than the actual battles."

This sounded like a game invented by Satan himself. "How many warriors would get killed each game?" I asked.

"Oh, the majority of them," Don said. "But anyone who survived eight straight matches could retire as a hero and become a TV commentator."

"What an honor," I said sarcastically.

Don smiled sadly. "I admit I watched part of the match when 'The Sweet Hooligan' and 'Johnny Electronic' were on opposing teams, each seeking to become the first-ever 'Eight Matcher.' Ironically, they ended up killing each other, but 89 percent of the nation watched, and soon new leagues sprouted up across the country to satisfy the legions who wanted their own chance to become a famous Eight Matcher."

"How depraved!"

Don nodded. "The people had forgotten God. The people who survived the war quickly became obsessed with vulgarity and pornography. People were so desensitized that Conquest actually seemed like family entertainment. TV became nothing but horrible shows promoting every sin imaginable. Many Latter-day Saints were enticed by these things and left the church. Thankfully the only TV station operating now is owned by the church. It's mainly used to update members on world events and for church broadcasts. I doubt there are many viewers besides those at New Jerusalem or at the temple compounds around the world."

I shook my head in sadness. "I'm not surprised society

ended up in the gutter. It was heading in that direction at the turn of the century."

"You're right," Don said. "Too bad it wasn't nipped in the bud. But anyway, back to Conquest. As I said, the game was a huge success, but the league fell apart after disasters began striking the cities where the teams were based. Las Vegas' downfall was the most horrifying, with all those millions of people trapped there without water."

"What happened?" I asked. "It was such a thriving city!"

"It all started with an earthquake beneath Hoover Dam. The dam split open, draining Lake Mead. Billions of gallons of water rushed away within three days. Without enough water, Las Vegas turned into a war zone within a week. People fled down I-15 in both directions, and some made it to California just in time to suffer through Los Angeles' series of earthquakes and fires.

"The thousands of Las Vegas residents that drove north on I-15 soon discovered the earthquake had closed up the Virgin River Gorge. Some people located the old original highway and made it to St. George, but the majority of the people ran out of gas and died in the desert."

I was speechless, so Don continued. "The ironic thing about Las Vegas' downfall is that one of the casino owners had earlier proclaimed he'd build the world's tallest building right there on the Las Vegas Strip. He named it 'The Tower of Babel.' Well, the building was nearly done when the earthquake hit, so now the world's tallest building stands in an abandoned city, just like the original Tower of Babel did. I think the Lord finally said, 'Enough is enough.'"

Chapter Three

We reached the end of a hallway and headed down a flight of stairs. "Aren't you worried you'll be stuck in Temple Square for several more years?" I asked.

Don chuckled at me. "I'm only here until the Savior's Second Coming. It can't be more than a few months away."

A few months?

"But how?" I asked. "The church seems to have fallen apart. I thought the church was supposed to grow and fill the whole earth. Where are all the members?"

Don glanced back at me with a slight grin. "Emma, I remember you as being somewhat of a scholar. Don't you know the answer to that?"

My mind was blank. "I guess not," I said with a shrug.

"Salt Lake isn't the headquarters of the church anymore," he said. "New Jerusalem is where all the action is."

New Jerusalem! Of course! The very words sounded futuristic and wonderful.

"Have you been there?" I asked excitedly. "Is it beautiful? Is my family there?"

Don held up his hands. "Hey, slow down! One question at a time." He took a moment to open a door, then he said, "Yes, I was there during the early construction phases of the temple complex. It's so glorious and delightful that it's hard to describe. Millions of Saints have gathered there, and the city itself is now gigantic, with at least a million homes filling the surrounding countryside. In fact, my wife and children live there."

"I'm sure you miss them greatly," I said sympathetically.

"I do, but it's worth the sacrifice," he said. "My family is safe and strong in the church, and I'm where the Lord needs me right now."

We entered a living quarters that contained a bedroom, a kitchen area, and a room with a sofa and a TV. Don checked his watch. "I'm due to rotate with another missionary in five minutes.

There are 12 of us serving here, and at least four of us are on duty at all times. Let me check if one of the other men can cover for me while I get you situated. Go ahead and make yourself comfortable until I get back. There are vegetables in the kitchen."

He departed, and I took a few carrots out of the fridge. I saw the remote control, so I turned on the TV and settled onto the couch. A newswoman's face filled the screen, and there was a small logo in the lower-left corner that read, "KSL Satellite Superstation."

The newswoman shuffled some papers before saying, "The Israelis have somehow held off the latest massive assault against Jerusalem. We've learned 300,000 Arab soldiers stormed around the north end of the Dead Sea aiming to conquer Jerusalem, but their attack was reportedly thwarted by a massive tornado that swept down on them from a clear sky."

Footage was shown of a monstrous tornado moving slowly across a rugged desert region, along with scenes of wounded soldiers. Some were missing arms and legs.

"The Category F-5 twister stayed on the ground for 30 minutes and seemingly followed the army, killing at least 250,000 soldiers and severely injuring the remaining 50,000. The Israeli Army then destroyed the surviving troops through the use of tanks and land-to-land missiles."

Don had returned, and he took a seat beside me on the couch. "Those guys are having too much fun," he said with a bemused smile. "Too bad the world can't accept the power of God, rather than brushing off all these miracles as strange weather incidents."

"Who's having fun?" I asked. "Those soldiers were in misery."

"I'm talking about the two apostles in Jerusalem," he said. He grabbed a Church Almanac off a table and opened it to a group photo of the Quorum of the Twelve Apostles. He pointed to two men. One looked about 65, while the other one appeared to be in his early 50's.

"These two have been in Jerusalem for just over three years, preaching the gospel and basically saving Israel from destruction through the use of the priesthood," Don said. "Without their intervention in behalf of the Lord, those northern countries would've crushed Israel to dust by now."

I tried to read who the men were, but Don held his hand over the names. "Come on," I pleaded. "Let me know who they are."

He shook his head. "It's best if you don't know. They were both born within a few years of us, and I actually was in the same stake with the younger one for a while. So if you eventually return to your proper time, you're likely to cross paths with them."

"Oh, I'd never say anything..."

Don raised a hand to stop me in mid-sentence. "It'd be too easy for you to approach one of them at a fireside and casually say, 'Did you know you're one of the prophets who'll preach in Jerusalem prior to the Second Coming?' It is prophesied that they'll finally be killed after three-and-a-half years in Jerusalem, and their deaths will help usher in the Second Coming. So it's a heavy burden they carry, and it's not something they need to know about until they receive their callings—and neither do you. "

I pouted a little, but I saw his point. "You're right. So these two have been over there for three years?"

"Yep, and they keep getting more creative. All they want is for the people to listen to the gospel of Jesus Christ, but the people's hearts have grown cold and merciless. So now the apostles' main goal is to hold off those armies until the time of the Savior's return."

"They seem a bit outnumbered," I said. "What is it? Two against 200 million?"

"The Lord has given them power to control the elements, so they're doing just fine," Dad said. "My favorite tactic they've used so far is when they sent hurricane-force winds against a huge squadron of enemy aircraft. The wind and the planes met right over the Sea of Galilee, and within minutes there were dozens of expensive planes plunging straight into the water. Today's tornado was pretty impressive, though."

"Doesn't the opposing army realize who's behind all this?"

"Believe me, the leaders of the invading armies know who's holding them at bay, and they've tried almost daily to kill the apostles, but obviously none of the attempts have succeeded. And they won't, either, until the appointed time."

Don went to the fridge and got his own handful of carrots, then I cautiously changed the subject. "What can you tell me about my family?"

"I'm afraid not very much," he said with a sigh. "I moved to northern California after college, so I only talked to Doug on rare occasions. I came back to Utah when World War III started, and I saw Doug briefly. He was still in Utah County, since Becky was too sick to make the journey to Zion."

"Becky?" I asked. "Who's she?"

Don gave me a funny look. "When did you start this latest time-travel thing?"

"I was on my way to the airport to see Doug arrive home from his mission."

"That's right! I wasn't even home from my mission yet," Don said. "So you don't know about anything that's happened in the past few decades?"

I shook my head, and Don laughed heartily. "How can I begin to explain what you've missed? Of course, the next few months are going to be pretty exciting, too, with all the prophecies coming together..."

I grabbed his arm. "You didn't answer my question. Who's Becky?"

Don collected his thoughts. "Oh, sorry. She's Doug's wife, but as I said, she was very ill when I last saw her. That's been a few years ago, right before 'The Big One' hit this valley."

I nodded. "From the appearance of some of the buildings, I figured a strong earthquake had struck Salt Lake."

He stood and motioned for me to follow him. "Actually, several large earthquakes have occurred. Let me show you the damage. It'll shock you to see the changes."

Chapter Four

We exited the east gates of Temple Square and crossed the pedestrian plaza to the Church Office Building, where Don took out a key and unlocked the door. The building was dark and empty, but Don flipped on some lights and led me to an elevator. We soon found ourselves on the west side of the 26th floor's observation deck. The valley's appearance *was* shocking. The most noticeable feature was how far the Great Salt Lake had receded. It was barely visible on the horizon. "What happened to the lake?" I asked.

"It has hardly rained or snowed here for two years. Plus, any river water has been diverted to help people survive," Don said. "The lake is now only about 20 percent the size it was in the year 2000."

I also noticed that nearly all of the valley floor was covered with subdivisions, but there weren't many signs of life beyond the downtown area. Also, the only trees I could see were on Temple Square or growing on the Conference Center's roof. Otherwise, there wasn't a single tree within miles.

"What happened to the trees?" I asked.

"We used them to build homes for people," Don said. "When all the riots and civil disputes erupted in the rest of the country after World War III ended, hundreds of thousands of people fled to Utah for safety. The Saints built homes for the new arrivals as fast as possible, and soon the entire Wasatch Front was bursting at the seams. Most of those last homes they built aren't much better than an old pioneer cabin, since no one had gas and oil to run any machinery. But the people were grateful for a roof over their heads, and they were very humble and teachable. A great majority joined the church."

I gazed again at the valley. "That is a ton of houses! But where is everyone?"

"When we'd nearly reached our limit, the prophet announced it was time to establish New Jerusalem at Independence, Missouri," Don said. "A few specially-called groups had already quietly journeyed there and got the city underway, and the time had come for a general gathering to Zion. Within three years most of the faithful Saints had moved there."

Don took my elbow and guided me to the east side of the observation deck. I gasped in surprise to see landslides and huge crevasses covering the mountainsides. One very deep, 150-foot-wide gash ran all along the foothills. I could see places where houses were teetering above the crevasse, and I'm sure many homes had been swallowed up. "That must've been quite an earth-quake," I said.

"You're looking at the handiwork of 'The Big One,'" Don said. "The Wasatch Front had experienced a few jolts in the 5.0 to 6.0 range every few months. These quakes worried everyone, but then the geologists started saying the worst had passed. But about a year after the prophet's general call to gather to New Jerusalem, this quake struck. It measured 7.3 on the Richter Scale and killed thousands. It's a miracle this building didn't topple, but the earth-quake's seismic waves skipped over Temple Square."

"Wow, I can't believe how the quake rearranged the foothills," I said.

Don gazed somberly at the mountains. "When the call came to move east, many wealthy Saints refused to go. They knew we'd be living the Law of Consecration in New Jerusalem, and they didn't want to share their possessions. They'd tolerated tithing, but most of them had refused to follow the prophet's counsel to assist the poorer Saints. Instead, these supposed 'Saints' stayed tucked away in their mansions and drove their fancy cars and lived the high life. As you know, there's no longer any electrical service or gasoline in this city, so I hope they're enjoying themselves."

I shook my head. "From what I've seen, the only ones having fun are those nuts in the homemade chariots. They nearly ran me over!"

"That's a crazy group," Don agreed, "but unfortunately, that's the cleanest entertainment in town these days. Which reminds me—beware of the followers of Sherem. Don't let them mislead you."

"Is Sherem a person? The name sounds familiar."

"Sherem was a Nephite apostate who's mentioned in the Book of Mormon," Don said. "Now we've got a modern-day Sherem. His real name is Larry Campbell, a former attorney who served time in prison for fraud. He now teaches what the original Sherem taught. He's the biggest con artist I've ever seen, but people have flocked to his teachings. He has deceived even the very elect."

Don now led me to the north side of the observation deck. He pointed up the hill to the State Capitol Building, which gleamed like new.

"That's Sherem's new hangout," Don said. "When the government fell apart, he moved in and cleaned it up. Living there has given him some undeserved credibility."

"What does he teach that could be so enticing?" I asked. "I mean, compared to the eternal promises the church offers, there doesn't seem to be any comparison."

"Sherem's teachings appeal to those who don't want to sacrifice anything," Don said. "To stay with the church requires a long journey to New Jerusalem and obeying the commandments. But Sherem teaches that Salt Lake is still the gathering place of the righteous, which is appealing to those who are comfortable here. Of course, his teachings also condemn marriage and sexual abstinence. Anyone looking for 'free love' can find it in Sherem's church. It feels wrong to even call it a church. It's more like a brothel."

I peered at the Capitol Building. "It sounds a lot like 'The Great and Spacious Building' to me."

Don laughed. "That's a good description. Someday Sherem's church will fall, but right now it's doing pretty brisk business."

He checked his watch. "I'm sorry, Emma, but I've got to get back to my shift. Brother Nielsen said he'd cover for me, but he needs his sleep. You're welcome to stay with us, but surely you have other plans, don't you?"

I would've been content to stay there in the safety of Temple Square, but I knew I was on an errand, despite my fears of returning to the crazy outside world. "I'd better leave," I said softly. Don nodded knowingly.

"I feel my errand here probably involves my family," I said. "Is there a way to safely reach Springville?"

"You're in luck," Don said. "The church repaired a set of railroad tracks after the earthquakes, and we have a freight train that takes supplies to each of the temples in this area. The train passes through Springville on its way to the Manti Temple, and I think I can convince them to take you along."

After all I'd seen in the past two hours, I had a hard time picturing a train casually rolling along in this environment—especially without a power source. "How does the train run?" I asked. "Doesn't it need fuel?"

Don pointed at the haze-shrouded sun. "All the energy we need is right there."

"The train is solar-powered? That's great!"

Don smiled. "Yep, the solar panels are embedded in the train engine's roof. We would've starved by now without a way to bring food in. Your timing is good, because our weekly delivery from Thanksgiving Point arrives tomorrow at noon. You can catch a ride with them."

"Is it safe to travel among these people?" I asked. "The ones I've seen so far would love to rob a train."

"That's why the train is armor-plated. Besides, once the train reaches 40 miles per hour, no one dares get in the way."

Chapter Five

Don escorted me back to the living quarters, and he showed me a pile of newspapers on a shelf. "I traded a lady some canned tomatoes for these one day at the north gate," Don said. "She was selling everything she owned just to feed her family. I figured these old copies of *The Deseret News* would someday make an interesting scrapbook. It's the only newspaper in the world that has continued to publish every day, even during the worst parts of World War III. Of course, now it's based in New Jerusalem."

Don said he'd see me later that night, then he exited the room to take over for Brother Nielsen. I sifted through the newspapers, and I could write a whole book just on the mesmerizing stories that lay before me. The articles seemed like a collection of fictionalized worst scenarios, except they were true.

Among the early 21st Century's startling lowlights: Continual warfare in Europe and Asia. Mob rule and civil war throughout North and South America. The collapse of the federal government. Washington D.C. abandoned. Tornadoes scouring the Plain States' major cities. Powerful hurricanes sweeping inland along both coasts and into the Gulf of Mexico almost weekly.

The most entertaining article, though, described several nudist colonies that had sprouted up on the shores of Lake Powell. The Glen Canyon Dam had survived the earthquakes, although it no longer produced electricity, and Lake Powell had become a popular spot for "naturalists" who survived mainly on fish. I winced at the carefully edited pictures of some badly sunburned people who really should've put on a swimsuit.

On a more somber note, one amazing front-page photo showed New York City completely engulfed in flames. The Twin Towers' blackened shells rose above the inferno.

I was reading intently about the destruction of Boston when Brother Nielsen entered the room. "These stories are almost unimaginable," I told him.

Brother Nielsen shrugged. "I guess you were too young to

remember, but when the economy collapsed after the war, it was like a dam bursting," he said. "When everything broke loose it rippled down from the highest levels of government to the smallest cities. Combined with the natural disasters, anarchy ruled for several months."

"I can't fathom that," I said. "Wasn't there some kind of warning?"

Brother Nielsen gave a patient smile. "The prophets told us for years to prepare for such events, and most of the Saints finally listened. The world ignored the prophets' pleas, of course, but the Saints were ready, and these mountains were the best place in the world to be during the worst destruction. This is still the second-best place on earth to live."

• • • •

I slept quite soundly on the couch that night, and at noon the following day Don escorted me to a gate in the electrified fence. It was near the Brigham Young statue in the plaza between Temple Square and the Joseph Smith Memorial Building. I was glad to see the statue had held up well, since Brigham's friendship had meant so much to me.

A three-car freight train had just arrived at the intersection of Main and South Temple. The train's cars were painted white, with a small window at the front of each one. A stocky, dark-haired man holding a pistol hopped off the train and walked up the tracks toward us. Several scraggly people observed us from nearby, but seeing the man's pistol kept them from approaching the train.

"Hello again, Jason," Don called out as he turned off the electricity and unlatched the gate. Jason waved, then he signaled for the train engineer to pull into the compound alongside the statue. Once the train was safely inside and the gate was closed, Jason came to our side. He looked to be in his mid-20s.

"Jason, please meet Emma, a close friend of mine," Don said. "She needs to find her family in Springville, and we're hoping she could ride along with you."

Jason stepped forward and shook my hand, but he seemed reluctant to help. "Is this a church-related matter?" he asked.

Don nodded. "She has a special errand to perform there."

Jason rubbed his chin. "Well, we'll be empty after

unloading your supplies, so we'll need to stock up again at Thanksgiving Point before going anywhere else. We'd planned to go to Manti tomorrow, but maybe we can squeeze it in later today."

Jason faced me and asked, "Would you be willing to help us pick fruit and vegetables this afternoon?"

"Certainly!"

"Then it's a deal."

Jason then introduced me to his co-workers, Ron and Ben, who were obviously father and son. Then we got to work unloading about 10 boxes filled with fruits and vegetables from the train's middle car.

"Do you go through this much food each week?" I asked Don.

"Yes, but we're hardly the biggest eaters. At some of the less-persecuted temple compounds the missionaries are allowed to have their wives stay with them, and those places use double or triple the food we use."

We carried the boxes into the Joseph Smith Memorial Building, then Don escorted us back to the train, where I gave him a hug good-bye.

"Thanks for getting me started on this little journey," I said. "I don't know what awaits me, but I doubt it'll be boring."

"Things haven't been boring around here for quite a while," Don said with a smile. "Be sure to say hello to Doug when you see him."

Jason escorted me to the train's caboose as Ron and Ben entered the engine. Through the window I saw Don pull out a pistol, turn off the electric fence, and nudge the gate open enough to let us through. The train rocked forward, and we followed a set of tracks that had been hammered right into Main Street's pavement, not far from the light-rail tracks. I looked nervously up at the teetering, crumbling skyscrapers, and Jason chuckled at me. "Don't worry, nothing has fallen onto the tracks for several months," he said. His words weren't very comforting.

We turned west on 200 South and soon linked up with the original tracks beyond 400 West. Then we were cruising smoothly toward Utah Valley, and I stayed glued to the window. Salt Lake's suburbs looked like ghost towns. The few people I saw were sitting lifelessly in stairways or were scavenging through trash piles.

Within minutes I could see the Jordan River Temple off to

the right, but Jason didn't even look at it. "Don't you take food there?" I asked.

Jason gave me a curious glance. "I thought everyone knew what happened there," he said. We were now within a mile of the temple and I could see black streaks surrounding its windows.

"I can't remember the details," I said meekly.

Jason seemed to bristle at a distant memory. "Vandals marched right in there and looted the temple, then they burned as much as they could. The same thing happened a week later in Bountiful. Thankfully the church leaders took quick action to save the other temples and protect the food supply at Thanksgiving Point."

We approached the Point of the Mountain, and as we rounded a bend I could see a group of people blocking the tracks ahead. Jason saw them, too. He quickly picked up what looked like a short-wave radio and said, "Ron, let's give these people a chance to get off the tracks. Slow it down to about five miles per hour."

"Sounds good," Ron's voice crackled back. "I hate having to hit them."

Jason put the radio down and picked up a microphone. "Attention!" Jason's voice boomed from a hidden outside speaker. "We don't have any food on the train. For your own safety, please get away from the tracks. Have a nice day."

I peered out at the hungry, poorly clothed families as we passed by them. "Have a nice day?" I asked incredulously.

"I'm just trying to be polite," Jason said. "These people know we sometimes drop off spoiled vegetables rather than throw them away. Unfortunately, there's never enough to feed them all."

We passed through the crowd, then picked up speed again as we crossed into Utah County. I searched the valley below for Utah Lake, but it now appeared to be two big ponds—one on the north near Lehi, and another far to the south at the base of West Mountain. Between these two "lakes" were acres of dried mud.

I was also surprised to see several housing developments along the west side of Utah Lake where I'd remembered only sagebrush. There had been a few communities sprouting up at the turn of the century, of course, such as Saratoga Springs and Eagle Mountain, but now there were thousands of homes west of the lake. It was a strange sight. I noticed several plumes of black smoke rising from West Mountain's northern foothills. I pointed and said excitedly, "Look, the mountain's on fire!"

Jason gave me a tired look. "Very funny," he said. "It's always on fire."

"I don't understand. Doesn't it ever go out?"

Jason now peered at me curiously. "You don't know who builds those fires?"

I shook my head, and he looked astonished. "Don't ever go near that town," he said cautiously.

"You mean where the smoke is coming from? There's a town there?"

"Yes," Jason said. "That's Lincoln Point, the most evil place in the valley."

"Thanks for the warning," I said, confused. "I'll stay clear of it."

We soon turned onto a spur of tracks leading to Thanksgiving Point, just north of Lehi. It was also surrounded by the same style of electrical fencing used at Temple Square. I noticed its golf course was yellow and dead. Golfing didn't seem to be a priority for people anymore.

A gate opened automatically for us a few yards east of the giant water tower that was still standing after all these years. We turned west at the dinosaur museum, and then Thanksgiving Point's agricultural area became visible. I marveled at several acres of crops. The trees and rows were filled with ripe fruits and vegetables, but I couldn't see anyone working in the fields.

"Do you three take care of this place by yourselves?" I asked.

"A few others also work here, but the top LDS horticulturists were asked to start the fruit orchards in New Jerusalem. The fruits and vegetables we harvest here basically produce by themselves. We have a few wells that we irrigate from, but rain has been almost non-existent, so it has been a miracle enough food is raised to feed the temple workers. We've been blessed."

Chapter Six

I spent over an hour helping Jason pick apples and pears, while Ron and Ben gathered tomatoes, corn and carrots. We filled several boxes and carried them to a handcart. Jason and I hauled our load to the train, then he signaled for the other two men to join us. Jason shielded his eyes and briefly glanced at the position of the sun. I naturally checked my wrist, but then remembered that one of the bikini babes had stolen my watch! I guessed it was probably 4:00 p.m.

"I think we've got enough sunlight left to drop Emma off in Springville and also make a delivery to the Manti Temple," Jason said to Ron. "That way, we'll be able to check the Springville depot on the way back to see if Emma really wants to stay there. What do you think?"

Ron nodded. "Sounds good, as long as we get out of Spanish Fork Canyon before dusk. The train's storage batteries have been on the blink lately, and I'd hate to be stranded there once the sun goes down. Lincoln Point's outer guards would surely find us. They attacked the train once in daylight, and I'd hate to see what they'd do in the dark."

Ben shuffled his feet. "You're right, Dad. I hate being in that end of the valley, especially this late in the day. Those Lincoln Point gangs will do anything to get our food."

I was intrigued by how scared they were of whoever lived at Lincoln Point. How could they be worse than the people I'd seen in downtown Salt Lake?

Jason then turned to me and said, "I'm nervous about you going into town alone. Are you sure you want to risk it?"

"If my family is there, it will be worth it," I said.

"OK, but we'll watch for you on the way back. We've been averaging about a three-hour round trip to Manti, so be at the depot if you don't want to stay there."

We quickly reboarded the train and headed south. The tracks followed the same railroad grade I remembered always

24

being used by regular freight trains. I looked again at I-15, unable to believe it was empty. Weeds were actually growing out of cracks in the freeway. As we neared Orem, Geneva Steel's silent smoke-stacks jutted into the sky to our right.

"My Grandpa Jack worked there for more than 30 years," I said. "I can't believe Geneva finally shut down."

"Did he ever work at the Missouri plant?" Jason asked.

"What do you mean?"

Jason shook his head slightly, a bit amused at how clueless I apparently was. "When the economy collapsed, Geneva Steel had no choice but to close its doors," he said. "But a good portion of the former Geneva employees journeyed with the Saints to Missouri. Outside Kansas City they built a small mill where they melted down and reused all the scrap metal in the area. That mill eventu-ally produced all of the steel that was used to build the New Jerusalem Temple complex and other major buildings in Zion."

"Really? Who would've thought it!"

We passed the crumbling buildings of Utah Valley State College and soon crossed under the freeway. When we emerged on the other side, everything seemed coated in silt. A path for the train had been cleared through piles of dried mud that'd been washed against the side of the train tracks.

"Whoa! Did a flood hit here?" I asked.

Jason gave me a funny look. "Of course there was a flood," Jason said. "Surely you've heard about the Deer Creek and Jordanelle flood disaster?"

I shook my head. "Sorry, I wasn't here at the time."

"It was pretty wild," Jason said. "Just look! You can see the damage all that water caused when those two dams collapsed after a major earthquake. The water rushed down the canyon, wiped out downtown Provo and flooded most of those new cities on the west side of the lake. The East Bay business district literally became the East Bay. Most of The Provo Town Centre mall floated halfway to Spanish Fork."

"I hope nobody was killed," I said.

"The initial wall of water killed hundreds of people in Provo and parts of Orem, but very few died elsewhere," Jason said. "The water quickly began draining down the Jordan River toward the Great Salt Lake, so parts of Salt Lake were flooded, too. The Jordan River looked more like the Mississippi River for a few days."

We reached southern Provo and passed under the University Avenue overpass at 600 South. I could see a watermark about 10 feet off the ground. I caught a glimpse of what remained of the East Bay shopping area. It had dried out, but now it was a collection of abandoned, half-buried buildings.

We traveled along the base of Ironton Hill, and within minutes we reached the outskirts of Springville. "Is there any chance my family still lives here?" I asked.

"I think most of Springville's citizens moved to New Jerusalem, but about 1,000 people stayed."

"I can't imagine why anyone would've chosen to remain," I said, peering at the abandoned homes on the city's west side.

Jason shrugged. "People mainly stayed out of selfishness or laziness. A lot of the citizens realized if they stayed, they'd be able to move rent-free into the homes the other Saints were leaving behind. All along the Wasatch Front it has been a repeat of when the Saints left Nauvoo in 1846. The people who stayed behind swooped right into the best homes."

"How do these people survive?" I asked. "Thanksgiving Point seems to be the only food source I've seen."

Jason shrugged. "People grow small gardens and raise chickens," he said. "It's a meager existence, but they somehow stay alive. The life expectancy here is much shorter than it used to be, though."

Ron brought the train to a stop at a small depot at 400 West and Center Street. "Good luck, Emma," Jason said as he opened the door. "I hope you locate your family, but if they aren't here, meet us back at this station in about three hours."

I thanked him, hopped off the armored train, then cautiously began walking through my hometown. A few filthy children ran out of a nearby home to gawk at the train, but they ignored me. I felt a sadness well up in my heart as I walked east on Center Street and saw the neglected yards, abandoned vehicles and run-down homes.

As I approached the City Park I was greeted by a rusty collection of carnival rides. Apparently the City of Fun Carnival had made one final appearance in Springville before its owners abandoned the business right in the middle of Center Street. The Ferris Wheel had toppled over, knocking down a traffic signal and partially blocking Main Street, while the cars of the Tilt-A-Whirl looked rusted into place.

I saw a small child peek out at me from the entrance of the House of Terror, but a woman quickly pulled the child back inside. Judging by what I'd seen of Springville in the past ten minutes, a spook alley was one of the better places to call home.

The rusting rides blocked the road, so I tried to find the sidewalk somewhere in the tall, dry grass. I then stopped in dismay as I saw the condition of the city library. It was heartbreaking to see every window had been smashed. And even worse, people were inside roasting a chicken over a pile of burning books!

I looked across the park at the police and fire station, but the building had buckled in half, probably during one of the earthquakes. I realized I was in a city without law enforcement. I felt as if 100 eyes were watching me. I hurried past the carnival rides, crossed Main Street and jogged up Center Street toward my parents' house. I paused long enough to peer over the bridge railing where Hobble Creek once ran, but now only layers of gravel remained where a stream had trickled steadily for hundreds of years.

I walked out into Center Street, feeling safest in the middle of the road. I admittedly dawdled along, absorbing all the changes that had taken place. Nearly 45 minutes had passed by the time I reached 300 East, and I was still a couple blocks from my parents' home. Then a disturbing sight greeted me. The Center Street Church, the LDS chapel where I'd attended meetings throughout my life, was in disrepair, and now posted on the door was a homemade sign that read in big letters:

The Church of Sherem.
Join us! We hold the secrets
to enlightenment and peace.

It angered me greatly to see such a sacred place desecrated, but the church seemed empty, so I turned the corner and soon approached my parents' home on 100 North. My heart raced as I saw Doug's rusted yellow Volkswagen parked on what remained of the front lawn. The car was now up on cinderblocks and didn't have any tires. There was also a pile of car parts nearby that looked like the roof and sides of a minivan, along with an engine, gas tank and exhaust system. Somebody had stripped that vehicle to the bare minimum.

As I surveyed the yard I truly hoped my family wasn't still living there. I prayed they'd stayed faithful and had moved on to New Jerusalem. I couldn't blame them for leaving Doug's Volkswagen, though.

Chapter Seven

I was certain my family was gone when I spotted two shirtless, filthy men sitting on my mother's porch taking turns drinking a brown liquid out of a Mason jar. The men were laughing and cracking crude jokes. I didn't want to be seen, so I darted behind the Volkswagen.

"Hey, I just saw a pretty girl," I heard one of them say, but his friend just laughed at him. "There's no pretty girls left in this town, Lem," the friend snorted. "You're drunker than I thought!"

Lem wouldn't let up, though. "I saw a pretty girl! She's behind the car!" I heard him get out of his chair and come my way. Oh great! I decided to take action rather than cower helplessly. As he approached, I jumped out in a karate stance and shouted, "Stop right there! You two are trespassing!"

Lem nearly jumped out of his boxer shorts—which was all he was wearing—and stumbled backward. "Don't hurt me," he said in a drunken drawl. "No one was living here, so we thought it was available."

I glared at him. "This is my parents' house," I said nervously. "I grew up here."

"I don't think so," Lem said, regaining his courage. "We've lived here for four years, and no one has ever asked us to move."

I realized Lem was probably telling the truth, since it appeared my parents had headed to New Jerusalem. These men made me very uncomfortable, and I decided to leave immediately.

I looked past Lem at my favorite old maple tree in the corner of the yard. The tree's biggest limbs had been cut off and the tree was nearly dead. Then I noticed the outline of a wide trench that'd once been dug around the tree and then refilled.

I felt queasy, realizing what that trench meant. I'd once agreed with Doug to bury a message 10 feet from the tree if I was ever sent on another errand for the Lord. Doug and my parents must've searched fruitlessly for a message from me, in hopes of discovering where I'd ended up. Leaving a message now would obviously be a waste, though, since I'd gone forward in time instead of back.

Something else also caught my eye. I walked cautiously around Lem and went to the tree. Words had been carved in the tree bark! It had been carved within the last few years, but the tree was beginning to heal itself, making the letters hard to read.

"Did you carve this?" I asked Lem.

He shook his head. "An old man came about three years ago and starting stabbing the tree. We finally chased him off with a stick."

I ran my fingers across the indentions, trying to decipher them. "What did the man look like?" I asked.

"A typical old man," Lem said with a shrug. "What was he, Barry? At least 70?"

Barry nodded and described the man to me. My excitement grew as he clearly described an older version of my father! I took a step back from the tree, and the carvings began to make sense before my eyes. It read:

Emma, go to Provo Tem

My heart beat wildly. Dad had been able to carve just enough. My excitement turned to worry, though, as I turned back around to see Lem and Barry slowly approaching me with lustful eyes.

"Get away from me," I said firmly.

"Come on, let's have a little fun," Lem said wickedly.

"Not with you!" I retorted.

Lem grunted, then took another swig from his jar before saying, "Maybe you won't have a say in it."

He lunged at me, but I darted around him. Barry blocked my path to the sidewalk, and I didn't dare go into the house. I could only guess the horrors I'd face if they trapped me inside. So I scampered up the hood of the Volkswagen and stood on top of the car. The paint cracked as the roof buckled a little, and I was afraid it would collapse. The men stood on opposite sides of the car, enjoying this little game.

"What you're trying to do is wrong," I said as calmly as I could, but they just laughed at that.

"Nothing's wrong anymore," Barry said. "Haven't you

heard the news? It's OK for us to just do what feels good."

I shook my head in frustration. "You two are sick!"

Lem suddenly grabbed my ankle, but I shook loose and leaped off the Volkswagen. Lem tried to catch me, but I put my right knee in his chest. We toppled to the ground and I heard a couple of bones crack within him as we hit. Lem groaned and his eyes rolled back into his head.

Lem had dropped his jar of homemade brew during our tussle, and I quickly picked it up and flung the remaining liquid into Barry's face as he came around the car.

"My eyes! Oh, they're burning," he screamed.

"Sorry if I hurt you," I said, amazed I had escaped. "I just took your advice and did what felt good!"

Barry cursed at me as I ran down the street, but he didn't seem to be following me. I was going back to the train depot. This just didn't feel like my hometown anymore.

Chapter Eight

As I sprinted back to Center Street I was as frustrated as I'd ever been. Acting out your passions seemed to be the normal thing to do among these people, no matter who it hurt. And Brother Nielsen had said Utah was the second-best place on earth! That was truly terrifying.

I heard piano music filtering out of the Center Street Church as I passed it again. The song being played was sinister and fast-paced, and it bothered me to hear such music coming from that wonderful building. I left the street and marched through the church's front door, which was now propped open. I entered the chapel and saw a few people sitting in the pews, but several middle-aged couples were dancing lewdly in the aisles and on the stage. It was grotesque.

I glanced at the north wall of the chapel and saw that the four murals I'd admired each Sunday growing up were still there. I knew these murals were the actual plaster casts of the bronze plaques that were placed on four sides of the Hill Cumorah monument. They depicted sacred events of the church's restoration, but now they were partially covered by graffiti. I could barely control my anger that such beautiful pieces of art had been desecrated.

On the stage I saw a hefty woman with waist-length hair playing her heart out on the piano. She wore a brightly colored low-cut dress and a tiara on her head. I guessed she was the leader of this disgusting group.

I skirted my way around some gyrating dancers and climbed the steps to the stage. A feeling of righteous indignation welled up in me as I slammed my hand down on the piano. "Would you please stop that racket?" I shouted. "This is a holy place!"

The woman stopped playing and glared at me. Her eyes frightened me, and I backed away a foot or two. "Um, that type of music doesn't belong here," I said less confidently.

"And who are you?" she said tauntingly. "I'm the priestess of this congregation, and I'll play whatever I want!"

We paused, eyeing each other carefully. The other people in the room were now watching our conversation. This woman reeked of the same homemade beverage that Barry and Lem had been drinking, and she let out a small burp. But there was something very familiar about her, and she seemed intrigued by me, too.

"I ought to throw you out of here on your head, but I've got a question for you," the woman said in a slurred voice. "Are you a Dalton? You look like a girl I grew up with, although she'd be in her fifties by now. I know the little wench got married, and she probably ran off to Missouri with the rest of the Mormons. I can't remember her married name, but her first name was Emma."

I was caught off-guard. Who was this woman?

"Yes, I know Emma," I said cautiously. "Why?"

"Oh, we used to go dancing together, but then she started thinking she was too good for me," the woman said angrily. "Next time you see her, tell her she really missed out! Look at how happy my followers are!" She waved her arms at the overweight, underdressed group below us. I'd never seen such a pathetic collection of people in my life.

"I'll be sure to tell her," I said, still unsure who this frightening woman was. "And might I ask your name?"

The woman puffed out her chest and proclaimed, "I'm Serena, the High Priestess of the Church of Sherem."

I'd seen that arrogant profile many times during my teenage years, and my mouth fell open in astonishment. "No you're not," I said. "You're Angie Newman."

The woman's eyes quickly darted across the congregation. "Shut up," she hissed. "That name no longer exists. Your self-righteous relative wasn't any fun to be around, and you're even less charming. Now get out of here!"

She resumed her maniacal piano playing, and her followers began prancing around again. The spirit in the chapel felt dark and oppressive, and I quickly fled the building.

My anger was gone, and now I just felt depressed. Angie had been one of my best friends during high school, but we'd gone our separate ways after graduation when she started seeking for worldly excitement in her life. She'd obviously found it.

I felt I'd let her down, though. The woman playing the piano was just a hollow shell of my teenage friend. In fact, the woman I'd just seen was completely devoid of spirituality. I didn't see any chance she'd ever return to the church, and it hurt me deeply.

· · · · ·

I walked slowly back to the train depot, lost in memories of more pleasant times when Angie and I had been close. But my daydreaming was interrupted by a shout behind me. "Get back here, girl! You hurt Lem!"

I saw Barry jogging slowly down the street after me. He was out of shape, and I easily stayed about a block ahead of him. But as we passed the abandoned carnival, Barry's shouts brought people out from among the rusting rides. Once Barry saw he was attracting attention, his shouts became more confident.

"You can't escape, girl! We'll catch up with you!"

I nervously realized he was right. It'd only been about an hour-and-a-half since the train had left for Manti, and now I really needed some help. I tried to walk calmly to avoid drawing attention to myself, but I glanced down at my red sweater and blue jeans and realized I was dressed like a queen compared to the rest of these people.

By the time I reached the station about 20 people were following me, more out of curiosity than in heed to Barry's shouts. But now I had nowhere to go. Beyond the tracks were just more abandoned, collapsed houses.

Barry finally got within a few feet of me. "You're going to pay, girl! My best friend is hurt, and my eyes burn."

"Don't blame me," I said angrily. "If you two had any morals, everything would be fine."

Barry took a few steps toward me, and I backed up to the edge of the station platform, unsure how to defend myself.

Honnnkkk! Honnnkkk!

I glanced up the tracks. Hooray! It was the train—arriving caboose-first! Many of the people scurried away, but Barry barely glanced at the train as he maneuvered to grab me.

Crack!

The platform board at Barry's feet splintered into the air, and he jumped back. I saw Jason standing at the rear of the train with his pistol pointed at Barry's chest.

"Get away from her!" Jason shouted.

Barry froze in place with his hands in the air. "Don't shoot me! I wasn't doing nothing, man!"

The train slowed but didn't stop completely, so I grabbed a railing on the caboose and pulled myself onto its back steps. As soon as I was aboard, Ron cranked up the engine and we raced out of Springville.

"That was good timing," I said gratefully as Jason led me inside the caboose. "Like you said, my hometown has changed a lot since I was last here."

"I apologize," Jason said. "I should've never left you alone like that. We'd gone up the canyon for about a half-hour when Ron stopped the train just below the Thistle Landslide. He told us he had a strong impression you were in trouble, so he threw the train into reverse and we obviously made it back just in time. I was prepared to go looking for you."

"I did see some scary things in town, but it was worth the trip," I said thoughtfully. "I crossed paths with an old friend, which was an eye-opener. Angie has changed quite a bit."

"Do you see any sign of your family?"

"No, they're gone," I said. "Two drunks live in our house now." Then I remembered the tree carving. "There was something, though. Is there any chance of going to the Provo Temple?"

"Well, that's actually our new plan. Since it's getting too late in the day to travel through Spanish Fork Canyon safely, we're going to drop off these supplies in Provo."

"Great! I think we'll find my parents there."

Chapter Nine

We glided back along the tracks toward Provo. West of the Provo Cemetery was a switching area where we turned the train around. Then we followed a new set of tracks along Provo's State Street and onto 900 East. The effects of the flood were evident until about 700 North, where the road really begins to climb toward the temple. The solar-powered train seemed to struggle a little on this steep section.

"We'll really get flying on the way back down," Jason said. "This climb takes a while, though."

I didn't mind, since I got a good look at the BYU campus. The Wilkinson Center was dark, and it appeared a fire had ripped through the Hunter Law Building.

"Did the church try to fence off the campus?" I asked.

Jason shook his head. "After the flood hit, the buildings on campus were used to house the hundreds of families who had lost their homes. It was impossible to hold classes, so the university basically ceased to exist. When the call came for everyone to gather to Zion, the church didn't spend a lot of time preserving things. They did seal off the underground portion of the Lee Library, though. There's a lot of valuable information and artifacts stored away down there."

We soon approached the Missionary Training Center. It also wasn't fenced off. "I thought they would've protected the MTC," I said.

"The MTC was also filled with flood victims, which was fine, since missionary work basically stopped during the worst of the calamities," Jason explained to me. "A few families must still live there, because I sometimes see children running around outside."

The train turned east and headed up the hill toward the temple. The temple block was surrounded by the same electric fencing I'd seen at Temple Square.

"I'm glad the temples were saved," I said. "It would've been a shame to see them all destroyed."

"The temples are just taking a short break," Jason said. "As soon as the Millennium begins, these temples will be running 24 hours a day."

That was mind-boggling to me. "I thought the Millennium would be a time of peace and rest," I said.

"We'll get a rest from wickedness, but we'll all be busy doing the work of the Lord," Jason said. "There's still so much temple work left to do."

. . . .

An elderly man greeted us at the temple's electrified fence. He opened the gate and we chugged up the hill where the pavement used to be. The train stopped alongside where the fountain once flowed, and a dozen people came out of the temple to help unload the supplies. Jason went to organize them, but I stayed at the caboose window, searching the group for my parents. Most of the people were at least 50 years old. None of the faces looked familiar, and I disappointedly disembarked from the train. Jason was now inside the boxcar, and he tossed a box of apples to me, which I carried through the sliding glass doors. Like Temple Square, the Provo Temple also appeared to have its own power station.

I saw a gray-haired woman sitting in a chair a few feet inside the entrance. She clapped her hands when she saw me. "Hooray!" she exclaimed. "Emma, I knew you'd come today!"

I did a doubletake. *Mom?*

I looked into her eyes, and there was no doubt. I hurriedly handed the box of apples to someone else and clutched my mother's hands. "I'm so glad to see you!" I said breathlessly. "I've felt so alone."

Mom pulled me to her in a big embrace. She was very frail, but I felt comforted in her arms. She ran her fingers through my hair and said, "You're safe here, honey."

After a few moments, I pulled back from her. "Are you OK, Mom? You look like you're in pain."

"I ache everywhere, but I can still walk short distances," she said. "My body's just worn out. We've been through a lot the past couple of decades."

"Like what?" I asked.

She patted my hand patiently. "We'll talk about it tonight. I'll fill you in."

"Is Dad still alive?" I asked. "He carved the message in our tree, didn't he?"

"Yes, he carved the message, and he's very much alive," she said. "He's in the basement helping stack the supplies. Let's go find him."

I helped Mom walk through the lobby and around the corner to the elevator. "I know this sounds silly, but it seemed as if you were waiting for me at the door," I said. "How could you have known I'd be coming?"

Mom chuckled. "This whole conversation is in your book. You never gave a detailed time-frame, though, so I've waited anxiously at the door for two days now."

Her comment made no sense to me. I shook my head and said, "The only book I've written was about my journey to the 1860s."

"The only book you've written *so far*," Mom said slyly. "Don't worry, Dad and I will try to explain everything."

After a wonderful reunion with my father we went to their sleeping quarters, which was formerly a meeting room in the temple basement. "This isn't how I thought you two would be living just before the Second Coming," I said. "I was sure you'd either be living in New Jerusalem—or be dead."

They brushed off my impolite remark with a laugh. "I'm surprised I'm still alive, too," Dad said. "As for New Jerusalem, we spent some time there during its early stages before being assigned here."

My mind was racing as I struggled to piece everything together. So where was I—the middle-aged me?

Chapter Ten

My parents seemed to be on edge, as if they wanted to discuss something but couldn't quite bring it up. Finally Mom said, "Emma, aren't you curious about what Doug looks like now?"

I shrugged. "Sure! Is he still athletic?"

Mom took a framed photo off a nearby dresser and handed it to me. The photo showed a thirty-something couple posing with three young children.

Mom pointed to each one. "You surely recognize Doug, and that's his wife Becky. The children are Justin, Heather and little Daniel."

I gave a startled laugh. "Doug stayed in good shape, but where's his hair?"

"We're not sure if his World War II experiences caused it, but by age 30 he was going bald on top," Dad said.

I looked closely at Doug's wife, a beautiful dark-haired lady. "Don Fowers told me about Becky," I said. "He said she was very ill when he last saw her."

My parents looked grim. "Becky passed away just a few months after Don came through town," Mom said. "She had contracted a supervirus a few years earlier that no medicine could touch. She suffered greatly, but thankfully we could be here to help with the kids after she died, since Doug was on his mission."

I stared at them in astonishment. "Why would the church worry about missionary work at a time like this? Didn't Doug have enough to worry about?"

My parents smiled patiently. "We're glad to see you come to your brother's defense, but this was a call Doug never would've turned down," Dad said. "He's serving as one of the 144,000 High Priests that are scouring the earth one last time. It's a tremendous honor for him, despite the dangers he's certainly facing."

"I've missed so many things!" I exclaimed. "So where are Doug's kids?"

Dad shifted uncomfortably. "First of all, take a closer look at little Daniel."

I pulled the photo closer and was surprised to see that Daniel only had one arm! He had a nice smile, but I saw he also had some facial deformities. "Oh goodness," I gasped.

Dad put a hand on my shoulder. "Becky became pregnant right before she contracted the supervirus, so Daniel suffered its effects, too. We didn't think he'd even live beyond birth, but the little guy held on for three years."

A lump came to my throat. "He's dead?"

"Yes, but it was a blessing for him," Dad said. "Daniel was a wonderful boy. He hardly cried, and I could sense a great spirit was trapped in that crippled little body. Daniel never learned to talk, and I don't think he could see or hear very well."

Mom wiped away a tear and cleared her throat. "Thankfully, Grandpa and Grandma Dalton had stayed here while we helped establish Zion. Since they'd been temple workers here before the war, they just resumed their duties when we returned from the canyon refuge. They were a great strength to Doug and Becky during those hard times. However, when your dad and I returned from New Jerusalem two years later, your grandparents' health had really slipped. In fact, Grandma Sheila passed away within a month of our return."

I smiled sadly. "She'd always wanted to live until the Second Coming, and she almost made it! When did the others pass away?"

"Daniel and Becky both died within six days of each other a few months after Grandma's death," Mom said. "And then Grandpa Jack died of a heart attack the next month."

"Whoa, that's a lot of funerals in one year," I said.

Dad nodded. "It was difficult to lose them all so close together, but I suppose the Lord has put their talents to work in the spirit world."

I sat silently for a moment, trying to absorb what they'd told me. Dad then pointed to another framed photo on a shelf across the room. "Let's move on to another subject. Aren't you the least bit curious about the family in that picture?"

I put down Doug's family photo and retrieved the other one. It was a shock to my 22-year-old system. It was my family! Tad looked in good shape, although he'd lost some hair, too. Then I looked at myself. I looked cheerful, but I was also quite...chunky.

"Hmmm. Am I really this plump?"

Mom put her arms around me. "I knew you wouldn't like this picture," she said. "Who cares if you've filled out just a little? You've become a beautiful, healthy middle-aged woman who radiates happiness to those around her, especially when times are tough."

That comforted me a little, and I quickly moved to a happier subject. "Look at my kids!" I said excitedly, grateful to know I'd someday have children. "Two boys and a little girl—just like Doug had. That's kind of funny!"

"Yep, you both ended up with three children," Dad said. "But Doug's daughter came in the middle, while your daughter came last."

"What are my kids' names?"

"Your oldest child is David, named after Tad's ancestor—and your old boyfriend," Mom said with a grin. "Then a few years later came Charles, named after Tad's grandpa, and then at last came little Leah."

Tears came to my eyes as I heard Mom recite the names. I pictured the people my boys had been named after, and I could see a part of these dear men in their smiling faces. And I sensed that Leah had been named after my close friend, Leah Jensen.

"I always felt Leah would be a good name for a daughter," I said.

"She's a charming girl," Dad said. "You'd be proud of her."

I pondered for a moment. "So where am I now?"

"You mean the 'older' you?" Dad asked. "I suppose you've disappeared from your home in New Jerusalem, since you can't be in two places at the same time."

"But I don't remember living there..."

Dad shrugged. "I don't understand how it all works either, but the Lord does. And I'm sure your older version will return to New Jerusalem when your errand ends."

"I hope my family handled everything all right," I said.

"Don't worry, they've been expecting this," Mom said. "They'll take it as a wonderful sign. In fact, you've been expecting it yourself."

I raised my eyebrows in surprise. Boy, it was very easy to get confused when everyone else knew all the answers!

Dad walked to a bookcase that held several church-related

books. "We have much to discuss in a very short time, but first you've got some reading to do." He pulled three books off the shelf and handed the first one to me.

"I suppose you recognize this book," Dad said.

"Sure. I wrote it after my journey to 1868."

He then handed me a second book. "This is the book Doug wrote after his experience in the 1940s. You really need to read it. It'll help you catch up on a few things that occurred after your car wreck in Salt Lake. Doug waited for a few months before writing it, since you'd promised to help him. But you took a long time getting back, so Doug went ahead and wrote it."

Dad was still holding a third volume. I reached out for it, but he pulled it back. "This one isn't for you," he said. "No matter what, do *not* read it during your stay here."

"What is it?" I asked.

Mom came to my side and gripped my arm tightly, as if to stop me from grabbing the book. I could sense her anxiousness. "It's your account of the errand you're experiencing right now," she said. "But it would possibly destroy your mission here if you knew what lay ahead."

I felt weak and sat down on the bed. "I wrote that book, and yet I can't read it? Wouldn't that make everything easier?"

Dad sighed. "I doubt it. You'd avoid the tough situations and maybe make things worse, since the future isn't set in stone. If you read the book, it would alter what you've written anyway."

I threw my hands in the air. "I feel completely lost."

"Just read Doug's book tonight, then we'll answer any questions you have in the morning," Dad said. I nodded, and my parents each gave me a comforting hug.

"I love you so much," Mom said. "Things will work out."

They walked to the door, and I saw Dad holding that third volume. It angered me that Dad wouldn't let me read it, but now I see the wisdom in my parents' decision. Meanwhile, I propped up the pillows on the bed and quickly became absorbed in the dilemma Doug endured in 1944.

Chapter Eleven

I read Doug's book in about three hours, taking only a short break to eat when Mom brought me an apple and two pieces of wheat bread. Then I fell into a deep sleep on a couch in the hall. When I awoke several hours later, my parents were already gone, but they'd left a note telling me to meet them in the temple cafeteria around the corner.

I found my parents eating breakfast at a table with a man about their age. I joined them, and a woman brought me a plate of pancakes. I thanked her and began eating as Dad introduced me to their friend.

"Emma, I'm sure you remember Brother Newman," Dad said. I froze for a second, then swallowed what was in my mouth.

"Uh, hello. You're Angie's father." Then I turned to Mom and whispered, "Does he know who I am?"

Brother Newman overheard me. "I know your story, Emma," he said with a sad smile. "You and Angie were good friends in high school, right? Too bad it didn't stay that way. Angie has gone a bit astray."

I nodded. "In fact, I saw her yesterday at the Center Street chapel. She was playing the piano for a group of people. She scared me a little."

"I know what you mean," Brother Newman said sadly. "Did she recognize you?"

"She could tell I was a Dalton, which didn't help things. She seemed very bitter toward me."

"She's bitter toward everyone," Brother Newman said while rubbing his arms in frustration. "I don't know how I'll ever bring Angie back to the truth!"

I felt badly for him. I didn't want to open old wounds, but I desperately wanted to know more about Angie, who'd once been one of my best friends.

"Brother Newman, I knew Angie was struggling with a few things, but I never imagined she'd end up like this," I said. "What happened?"

"It just started with small choices," Brother Newman said slowly. "Once she began drinking, though, things really went downhill. She didn't hold her liquor very well."

He paused for a deep breath, then plunged forward. "She got pregnant when she was 20, but the father was out of the picture before the baby was even born. Then before her son was even a year old Angie met a hot-shot attorney at a Salt Lake nightclub. Within three months she'd moved from her Springville apartment into his mansion overlooking the University of Utah. He's the one who got Angie hooked on alcohol and drugs."

"This guy sounds like a real winner," I said wistfully.

"You can say that again," Brother Newman said. "He went to prison for fraud two years later, and he locked up all his assets, leaving Angie with nothing. From then on, she would live with any man that would support her. We soon lost track of her, but she came home for a while after the first big earthquake hit Salt Lake."

"What happened to her son?"

"We never saw him again. She wouldn't talk about him much, but it sounded like she'd let him run wild in the streets. Angie thought he'd joined a gang."

"How horrible," I said, genuinely saddened.

"It's been painful for us, but we still loved her and prayed for her."

"When I saw her yesterday, she called herself 'Serena, the High Priestess.' How did she come up with that name?"

Brother Newman frowned in disgust. "Her boyfriend gave her that title after he became a religious zealot while in prison."

"Hold on," I said. "Don Fowers told me about an ex-con who changed his name to Sherem and lives in the State Capitol. Is this the same guy?"

"Yes," Brother Newman said. "Good old Larry Campbell. He was a crook before he entered prison, but at least he wasn't crazy. I heard he got hit in the head with a pipe during a prison riot, and suddenly he felt obligated to call the Mormons to repentance. He started writing letters to *The Deseret News* asking the prophet to come to his cell and debate with him. The prophet politely declined."

"I'm sure the prophet had more important things to do," I said.

"That's for sure," Brother Newman said. "In fact, church headquarters had already shifted to New Jerusalem by the time Larry—or Sherem—got out of prison. Within months came that final devastating earthquake, and Sherem took up residence in what was left of the Capitol Building. He and his followers rebuilt it, and Angie was soon at his side again as his 'prophetess.'"

The whole story made me lose my appetite. "Then why is Angie in Springville?"

"From what I can gather, Sherem sent her on a 'mission,' but I think he's got such a harem of women at the Capitol now that Angie was basically booted out."

"She certainly wasn't happy when I saw her," I said. "Oh, it just makes me ache inside for her!"

"Me too," Brother Newman said. "That's why I volunteered to come back here from New Jerusalem. I couldn't just abandon her while there's any chance she'll rejoin the church. I've visited her a few times, and while she treats me politely, she's beyond the point of no return. I never thought I'd say that, but I'm afraid it's true."

· · · ·

After breakfast, I went with Mom to help dust the temple's sealing rooms. I could feel the Spirit of the Lord strongly. "I get such a wonderful feeling here," I said reverently.

"This is still the Lord's house," Mom said as she removed two dust cloths from her dress pocket. "We can't do ordinance work right now since we've run out of proxy names, so we're doing all we can to keep the temple sanctified for what lies ahead."

She led me through a doorway and said, "I thought you'd like to clean this room. Does it look familiar?"

I saw the altar in the center of the room and realized this was where Tad and I had been sealed together for eternity. "Oh yes, it's still as beautiful as ever."

I looked into a mirror on the wall. It reflected my image into a mirror on the opposite wall, making it appear as if my reflection traveled on for eternity.

I helped Mom dust the room for a few minutes, then she motioned for me to sit down next to her. "Emma, I have some things to tell you, but last night you were too frazzled, plus you first needed to read Doug's book. How are you feeling now?"

"OK, I guess. Can you explain why I'm here?"

Mom looked intently into my eyes. "You seem stable enough now," she said as she took my hand. "The reason you're here involves Doug's children—Justin and Heather," Mom said. "They've taken off on their own into the valley, and they might very well lose their souls if you don't help them."

"They're here in Utah?" I asked in surprise. "I figured you would've sent them to New Jerusalem."

"That was the plan, but getting to Zion isn't an easy trip," Mom said. "So the kids remained here with us after Becky died. The Second Coming can't be too far away, and we decided the kids would be better off staying here, rather than be sent to Zion on their own."

"What happened to Becky's family?" I asked. "Doug's book made it sound like the Browns were strong members of the church."

"They certainly were," Mom said. "They were all living in California when the first troubles started. Tex and Ingrid sent a letter to Becky describing some of the lawlessness taking place there, and they wrote that the whole extended family would all be heading to Utah within the week. But Hoover Dam broke the day after she got the letter. We never heard from the Browns again."

"Never?"

Mom shook her head. "They were probably killed in the madness that happened all along I-15. It was a terrible shock to Becky to lose her entire family, but she held her head high and never blamed the Lord. She knew they had lived righteously and that they'd see each other again in the next life. She just felt sad that her children would never know her parents or grandparents."

"How old are Doug's kids now?" I asked.

"Justin just turned 15, and Heather is 13," Mom said. "That's part of the problem. They've been so antsy to see the world—they've been living inside this temple compound year after year. Now they've taken matters into their own hands, and they couldn't have selected a worse time to go sightseeing."

"Did they leave any clue of where they might go?"

"We have a good idea, but let's go talk to your father," she said. "He'll explain the situation better than I can." Mom involuntarily shuddered. "I hate to imagine what those kids are going through right now. Would you be willing to go search for them?"

My stomach turned over as I thought of the frightening people I'd seen in Springville, but I quietly said, "Yes."

. . . .

We returned downstairs and a man told us Dad was outside pulling weeds in front of the temple. "We don't have enough water to grow flowers, but your father likes to keep those flower beds clean," Mom said. We exited the temple and saw Dad working next to the dried-up fountain. We approached him and Mom said, "Mark, Emma has agreed to help find the kids."

Dad got off his knees and embraced me. "Thank you, honey. This means very much to us. I don't think you understand what this will require, though."

We went down the hill a few yards and sat on a bench with a good view across the valley. Dad rubbed his eyes and took a deep breath. "Justin and Heather left here two days ago on their bikes," he said. "They often rode around the temple grounds, so we didn't think much of their absence until an hour had passed. That's when I found the note on our bed."

Dad pulled a piece of paper out of his pocket and handed it to me. I saw a message hastily scribbled on the page. It read,

> **Dear Grandpa and Grandma,**
> **Justin would be very mad if he knew I wrote this, but I didn't want you to worry. We're just going for a little bike ride to explore Springville. We've never seen the house where Dad grew up, but I think we can find it. We'll be back in a day or two.**
> **Love, Heather**
> **P.S. I packed lots of food for us. See you soon!**

I shook my head in disbelief. "I was terrified out there! If these two kids are as naive as you say, they could be in major trouble!"

"Believe me, I know," Dad said. "Springville was bad when I went to carve that message on our tree, and it's only gotten worse."

I chuckled. "I had a run-in with those two drunks that live

in our house. One of them will be hurting for quite a while."

"I didn't like that pair—they've let the yard go to pieces," Dad said with a grin. "Anyway, I immediately set out after the kids on another bike, but they had a big head-start on me, plus they're in much better shape."

"Was there any sign of them?" I asked.

Dad's face was suddenly grim. "I asked a man living in the old Springville Taco Bell if he'd seen two teenagers on bikes, and he pointed south, so I knew they'd passed through town. I pedaled down Main Street and saw a woman living in a camper in front of the burned-down Burger King. She told me she'd seen a well-dressed boy and girl ride by earlier that day, and they'd turned the corner at 400 South and pedaled west toward..." Dad choked up and couldn't finish the sentence.

"What is it?" I asked anxiously. "Where were they going?"

Dad raised his arm and pointed across the valley. I again noticed smoke filling the sky from a fire on West Mountain's foothills.

"Lincoln Point," Dad said hoarsely.

Chapter Twelve

Lincoln Point? Jason had described it as the worst place in the valley. Surely the kids wouldn't go there!

"Aren't they smart enough to stay away?" I asked.

"We warned them many times," Dad said. "Justin has always had a rebellious streak, though. I don't think Springville was ever his final destination. He's always been curious about Lincoln Point, and I'll bet he's been planning this trip for a long time."

"What about Heather?" I asked.

"She's a wonderful girl who trusts her brother too much," Mom said. "I'm sure as they approached West Mountain she was torn between turning back alone or staying with Justin. It appears she stayed with him."

I was getting very frustrated. "I know it's a dangerous place, but can't we just go there and demand they return home?"

"You don't understand, Emma," Dad said. "There aren't fences to keep people out of Lincoln Point, but there are 20 ruffians guarding every road to the city who use devious tactics. If you're young and attractive, they treat you like royalty and entice you to join them. But if you look even 25, they'll beat the living heck out of you. And I don't think Heather and Justin understand that once you're in Lincoln Point, their leader doesn't let you leave the city until you're completely brainwashed. That's what I fear most."

I was starting to have serious doubts about my commitment to find the kids, and it must've shown on my face. "Are you all right, honey?" Dad asked.

"Isn't there another way to save the kids?" I said. "Are you saying there aren't any adults there to supervise things?"

Mom and Dad half-smiled, despite the seriousness of the situation. "Let's get you packed," Dad said. "Then I'll tell you all about what to expect in Lincoln Point."

• • • •

Dad went to the cafeteria to fill a backpack full of food and water for me, while Mom and I returned to the bedroom. Mom looked at me then said, "Take your clothes off. The ones you are wearing are way too nice—the guards would strip you naked within seconds."

"Mom!" Her words shocked me. "I haven't showered since I arrived here," I said. "I already feel grungy enough."

Mom shook her head. "The kids at Lincoln Point haven't bathed in years, so don't pout. In fact, we'll need to dirty you up and hide your slender figure from those lunatics. You're much too pretty to go looking like that."

Then Mom paused for a moment with a far-off look. "Hold on. I think I've got just what we need."

Mom pulled out the dresser's bottom drawer and removed a folded-up piece of clothing. "Look familiar?" she asked.

I immediately recognized the pattern on the fabric. "Mary's dress!" I took it from her and carefully unfolded the dress Mary Dalton had loaned me the night I'd attended the "End of the Harvest Dance" in Heber with David North. I'd obviously never given it back, since that very night I ended up returning from 1868. I'd since held onto it as a keepsake.

"It's still holding up pretty well after all these years," I said happily. "What made you bring it here?"

"When we abandoned our house I couldn't bear to leave the dress there," Mom said. "It's a link to our family's past, and I knew it meant a great deal to you."

I held the dress to my face and breathed deeply. "I can almost smell the hay in Finity's barn."

"I guess you can keep your clothes on if you wear the dress over them. Put it on, then take a seat," she said. "Dad and I still need to fill you in on a few things."

• • • •

Dad soon arrived with my supplies. He put the backpack on the floor and took a seat across from me. "I don't really know how to explain what you'll find at Lincoln Point unless I start back at the beginning, just a few years after you disappeared."

I nodded. "That's fine with me. Don Fowers told me a few

things, but I can't quite piece everything together. So go ahead."

"Lincoln Point started out as just one of the many new communities that sprouted up on the far side of Utah Lake, but it had a better water supply than the others, with the Spanish Fork River running nearby," Dad said. "Soon hundreds of homes had been built along the lake and around the northern end of the mountain. The city also built a nice park and swimming pool in the middle of town that gave a great view of the valley. Most of the homes were occupied by young families, and they created a splendid little community."

Mom spoke up. "Doug and Becky were looking to buy a house there, but that's when the war started."

"Which war?" I asked.

"Well, it's now known as World War III, although at first it seemed to be just another squabble in the Balkans. We took one side, while Russia and China took the opposing viewpoint. That all became inconsequential when Russia launched a surprise attack against us. Several cities along the East Coast and in the Northeast were turned to rubble. We retaliated, and soon millions of people had been killed. The two sides finally quit firing bombs at each other, and it became more of a traditional battle right here on American soil. The Russian and Chinese armies occupied several areas of the United States, such as central California and the Southeast, but our enemies never reached the Great Basin."

"World War III," I whispered in shock. "How long did it last?"

Dad turned to Mom. "What was it, dear? About 13 months from start to finish?"

"Yes, that's when the Lord came to our aid," Mom said. "Just when it appeared all was lost, there were several natural disasters—such as massive hurricanes—that swept the enemy away. Also, groups of LDS men in several of the coastal areas left the safety of the tent cities to help drive off the remaining invaders. They called themselves 'The Elders of Israel,' and they truly played a key role in ending the war."

"So then what happened?" I asked anxiously. "The world obviously didn't return to normal."

"By this time, the European and Asian nations were in such disarray that their citizens turned on each other, and they basically destroyed themselves," Dad said. "The people that survived eventually joined together to form the huge army that is holding Jerusalem under siege."

My head was swimming. It sounded unbelievable. "Hold on. I'm having trouble keeping up with you," I said. "Let's keep it simple. Please just explain how Lincoln Point turned out so awful."

Dad grinned sheepishly. "Sorry, I got a bit off track, but not too far, because it was World War III that triggered everything else that happened—the rioting, the civil wars, the judgments..."

"Mark, just tell her how the war affected us," Mom gently interrupted.

"That's a good idea," Dad said. "Once the bombs started falling, all commerce and business obviously ceased, and grocery stores were stripped bare within hours. We had our food storage, of course, and we knew we'd be fine—if we could just avoid an assault from our unprepared neighbors."

Mom shook her head. "It was horrible, Emma. Within three days there were reports in town of starving people breaking into their neighbors' homes to steal their food. One man stabbed his best friend to death over a box of animal crackers!"

I was stunned. "This happened in Springville?"

"Yes, and also all over the world. Thankfully the church leaders were inspired to prepare in advance. Each stake had been assigned a 'gathering place' in case of such an emergency, and supplies and tents had been stashed at the gathering sites. Crops had even been grown and harvested at each site. Each ward had an emergency preparedness specialist who taught and organized us, and then we went about our daily lives, knowing that someday we'd have to actually put the plans into effect."

"How did you know it was time to evacuate?"

"When we heard news reports that bombs were hitting the East Coast, we knew it was time. You and Doug brought your families to our house, and we loaded up the trucks with as much food as we could haul. Then we headed to our assigned 'tent city' in Hobble Creek Canyon. Armed guards were stationed at the mouth of the canyon, and if you didn't bring supplies with you, you weren't allowed in."

"What about the older, poor people who might not have supplies?" I asked.

"The only other way into the canyon was to agree to live peaceably and share everything," Dad said. "Of course, most of the people who were unprepared didn't even think of going to the canyon. Most hid in their basements and watched CNN, but they starved within weeks."

"Didn't any of them figure out to go to the canyon?" I asked.

"A few later did, but hardly any of them would agree to follow our requirements. They just wanted a handout and then wanted to return to their homes. We'd tell them we truly didn't have food to spare, which caused them to shout and curse, saying we'd forsaken them. There were a few ugly incidents between them and the guards, but we'd expected that. It was hard to turn them away, but they'd had as much opportunity to store food as the rest of us."

Mom raised her hand. "That reminds me of an incident that happened right after the war started. A married couple came to the mouth of the canyon trying to trade 150 music CDs for a loaf of bread. It's sad to think how much food they could've bought with the money they'd spent on those CDs!"

"Everyone's priorities changed very quickly," Dad said. "One thing became painfully obvious—a year's supply of fancy clothes and computer games won't satisfy your stomach."

I pondered their words. "It's like the Savior's parable of having oil in your lamp," I said. "If you didn't have your own oil, you weren't allowed into the wedding party."

"That's right," Dad said. "That's how it was throughout the valley. The Saints in Mapleton gathered in Maple Canyon and over into Little Diamond, while Spanish Fork's members gathered in Diamond Fork Canyon. Payson's Saints gathered in Payson Canyon, and so on."

"Wasn't it a bit crowded?" I asked.

"Not really," Mom said sadly. "Fewer were prepared than you'd think."

Dad shifted in his seat and continued, "We stayed in the canyon for a full year, during which time a biological weapon went off near Hill Air Force Base. The church leaders warned us to stay in our tents at all times, and although we lost a few people to the 'desolating scourge,' as it was called, we were truly spared compared to the rest of the nation. These weapons were designed by the enemy to kill the people but preserve the cities. Even the Saints in rural areas who stayed in their homes suffered much worse than those of us in the camps."

"I'd always imagined dozens of atomic bombs wiping everything out if there was another war," I said. "Didn't any of them hit the United States?"

"A couple hit the East Coast, but curiously the enemy opted to mainly use their biological weapons. It soon became clear their goal was to occupy America, not destroy it. This certainly worked in our favor, because we didn't hesitate using atomic weapons on them."

"Even so, the biological weapons were terribly effective," Mom said. "The mountains helped shield us, but we still had to deal with many cases of the scourge. Black sores would form on people's hands or faces, then the poisons would spread throughout the body. In some cases the flesh would just fall off the bones."

"Stop!" I cried. "You're making me sick!"

"It *was* sickening," Dad said. "But it really happened. That's when Becky caught that strange viral disease. It wasn't the actual scourge, but it nearly killed her, and as we explained, it affected little Daniel."

"Wasn't it hard to spend a full year there?"

"There were some tensions, of course," Mom said. "But we learned how to share everything equally. It made us better people and prepared us for what lay ahead."

Dad nodded. "We heard over the shortwave radios that the war was over, but we still stayed in the canyon for a few weeks until the effects of the scourge were gone. Then we finally entered the valley again and reclaimed our homes. Very few people in the valley were still alive, but those that remained soon cleared out of our way and occupied the cities on the west side of Utah Lake, including Lincoln Point."

"Was our house still in decent condition?" I asked. "It looked pretty scary when I saw it yesterday."

"It'd been ransacked," Dad said, "but we wouldn't be there long, anyway. "

"Why not?" I asked.

Dad smiled. "It was time to establish New Jerusalem."

Chapter Thirteen

I was fascinated by what my parents were telling me, but they seemed eager to end the conversation and get me on my way. "I know it's time to start my journey, but please fill me in on what happened next, " I pleaded. "Don't leave me hanging like this."

Dad checked his watch. "All right. Besides, I guess it'll be safer if we don't approach Lincoln Point until sundown."

"We?" I asked in surprise. "Are you going with me? You said the guards killed older people."

"I'll escort you as far as I can," Dad said.

That comforted me a little, but I was still frightened. I pushed my fears aside, though, as Mom continued the story.

"Once we returned to the valley, the church leaders contacted other church 'tent cities' across the nation. The astounding news started to trickle in that New York and Boston were destroyed, and Washington D.C. had been abandoned. Earthquakes and riotings had finished off California's big cities, and the Midwest had been scoured clean by tornadoes and civil war. Then came the hailstorm that wiped out any attempts to grow crops that year. By now even our food supply was getting low. Then came the next challenge."

"What could be more challenging than that?" I asked.

"Well, thousands of good people, mainly women, had survived the disasters in the East, and they now felt prompted to gather to the Rocky Mountains," Mom said. "Within weeks they streamed into the Wasatch Front, and the church opened up their buildings to house them all. Thankfully we were able to grow crops again before our food completely ran out. Then a messenger from church headquarters knocked on our door. He handed your dad a shortwave radio and said, 'The prophet would like to speak with you.'"

Dad grinned at the memory. "The prophet cheerfully asked me, 'Brother Dalton, how are you feeling? Any aches or pains?'

"I told him I felt fine, and he replied, 'That's good, since I'm calling you to lead a group of Saints from Springville to help establish New Jerusalem.' He explained we would help lay the foundation for Zion's temple, and also lay out the streets, plant crops, build houses, etc. And then he said, 'Make sure Tad, Emma and their children join you.'"

I bolted out of my seat. "Wow! That's fantastic! Did we go?"

"Yes, and it was a glorious experience," Dad said. "Your family stayed there, but Mom and I returned to help Becky and the kids. Later, I was called as temple president, so everything has worked out."

It was a lot to absorb. Finally I said, "Speaking of Doug's kids, this brings us full-circle. Can you please tell me now what makes Lincoln Point worse than anywhere else?"

Dad smiled. "I guess we drifted from your original question. Well, there was another 'sifting' of the Saints, you could say. Most of the Saints eventually left for New Jerusalem, but some of the members who'd endured the tent cities now felt the Lord was asking too much of them. They said they'd sacrificed enough. They stayed here instead, which is ironic, because the lifestyle in Zion is now a hundred times better than it is here."

"Don Fowers said the same selfishness affected some members in Salt Lake," I said with a frown. "I don't understand why."

"There were various reasons," Mom said. "Some members stayed here because they knew the Law of Consecration was in effect in New Jerusalem, and they didn't want to share. They called themselves 'Capitalists' and thought they could rebuild these cities and live well, but it's hard to do when you reject the will of the Lord and lose His support."

"Whatever happened to those people who hadn't ever joined with the Saints—the ones who moved to the west side of the lake when you came out of the canyon?"

"Eventually, their children became teenagers who drove their parents out of town. The kids then formed their own little commune," Dad said. "These kids are now in their late teens and early twenties, and they've never been taught morals or religion."

"So it's no surprise how those kids turned out," Mom said. "These kids had watched their parents kill people over food! Their consciences aren't bothered by even the most vile and wicked things, and anyone who goes near their commune has almost no defense against their enticements. They even go into the other cities to recruit people to come to their 'playground.'"

Dad nodded sadly. "Anyone who enters Lincoln Point quickly becomes tainted." Dad paused and wiped tears from his eyes. "And that's where our precious grandchildren are—and where I'm asking you to go."

We were silent for a few moments, then Dad spoke again. "Emma, unless you go, Justin and Heather are doomed," he said with his voice cracking. "Like I said before, the future isn't written in stone. There's no guarantee you'll make it out of there alive. And if you don't, I suppose the life you've lived beyond age 22 would cease to exist. Are you willing to take the risk?"

I stared at the ground with my heart pounding. "Doug would do this for my children," I finally said. "Let's go."

Chapter Fourteen

Mom still insisted I needed to look less attractive to succeed, so we pulled my hair back into a ponytail and put a floppy hat on my head. When we went outside, Mom smeared mud on the dress and on my cheeks.

"Is this really necessary?" I asked.

"You'll thank me later," she said. "There's one other thing—maybe you should use a different name. Justin and Heather have an Aunt Emma, and they think of her as older and...heavier. I think your best bet is to seem like one of their peers."

I pondered a possible nickname, and then one I'd hated as a teenager came to mind. Doug had been a star athlete in high school and had earned the nickname "Double D," because of his initials. Well, some students thought it would be funny to start calling me "E.D." That somehow evolved into "Eddie," and I hated it, since it sounded like a boy's name. This didn't help my already low self-esteem during high school—but that's another story.

"Remember when people would call me Eddie?" I asked. "Maybe that name will sound normal in the bizarre place I'm headed."

My parents chuckled. "That will work great," Mom said.

We went to the temple entrance, where a pair of old Schwinn 10-speeds awaited us. We kissed Mom good-bye before coasting out the temple's main gate and down to 900 East. We saw very few people, and we rode along in silence toward Springville. I glanced up at the "Y" on the mountain, but after years of neglect the mountain's shrubbery had begun to reclaim the letter, so now the "Y" resembled a gray, thin wishbone.

Shadows slowly crept up the mountains, and soon we were riding in darkness. My spine tingled a few times as dark objects moved along the roadside, especially as we started a pitch-black climb up Ironton Hill. The moon was nowhere to be seen. Dad was handling the ride better than me and I finally puffed, "How have you stayed in such good shape?"

"I haven't owned a car for more than a decade, so I've walked or biked everywhere. Don't forget I've gone to Zion and back on foot, pulling our supplies in a handcart most of the way. I either had to toughen up or die."

"There still isn't an easy way to New Jerusalem?"

"Nope," Dad said. "The church certainly could make one— if they wanted to. But the trip to Zion is more a test of faith than anything else. If we operated a railroad, it wouldn't be much different than if Brigham Young had built a railroad to Salt Lake for the lukewarm Saints that stayed behind in Nauvoo."

"I see your point," I said.

"It's not easy getting there, but it's worth it," Dad said. "Zion is beyond description."

I hesitantly asked, "Do you ever get discouraged that you aren't there?"

Dad shook his head. "I miss the feeling of safety and the beautiful scenery, but we all have a place to serve in the kingdom, with a duty to fulfill. My only regret is letting Justin and Heather out of my sight. Even though you'd mentioned their disappearance in your third book, I felt if I kept a close eye on the kids, you'd never have to rescue them from Lincoln Point. Justin is tough to figure out, though. He's good at heart, but..."

"But what?" I asked. "Has he pulled stunts like this before?"

"Nothing this extreme, but he's always been a bit of a rebel. As a youngster he'd somehow climb onto the temple roof and have to be dragged kicking and screaming down the ladder. Then in the past few weeks I've seen him talking to some wild-haired kids down at the fence. I asked him to stop meeting with them, but he'd throw a tantrum and shout, 'Leave me alone! You're not my dad!' So he and I have had some arguments, and I'm afraid I pushed him into doing exactly what I'd tried to stop. I'm really worried what he might attempt in an 'anything goes' environment."

We reached the top of Ironton Hill and then coasted silently down into Springville. The city was quiet, but we stayed in the middle of Main Street just to be safe. You don't appreciate light poles until they no longer work.

The moon finally began to creep over Maple Mountain, and it provided just enough light to make me feel safe enough to speak again. "Dad, what is Heather like?"

"She's much like you," he said. "She's a polite, quiet girl

who doesn't deserve to be in this situation. I'm certain she had no idea where Justin intended to go. She's the one I'm most worried about, because she's so vulnerable. She must be terrified."

We passed the city park and abandoned carnival once again. I saw flames flickering through the broken window panes of the library. "You'd think they'd eventually run out of books to burn, wouldn't you?" Dad asked softly.

"It's too bad they don't read the books," I said angrily. "Maybe that'd help improve things."

Dad chuckled at me. "Reading's a lost art around here, Emma."

We crossed 200 South and noticed Central Bank's windows had been smashed. "I guess a vault filled with money doesn't buy much these days," I said.

"Not anymore," Dad said. "But it was neat to see the bank owners quietly give supplies to the city's younger families when times got tough."

We reached the corner of 400 South and Main Street about an hour after we'd left the temple. We braked to a stop and I gawked at the crumbling remains of Burger King, whose sign on the corner read, *"Managerial Position Available. Apply Within."*

I realized I was standing only a few yards from where I'd once entered the city's long-gone wooden gates with Brigham Young. I'd been so confused that day in 1868, but now I would've given anything to be back there.

Dad snapped me back to reality by putting his hand on my arm. "I can't go beyond this point," he said.

"Are you sure you can't come with me?" I pleaded.

"Sorry, but the first set of Lincoln Point guards usually camp just beyond the first overpass. Your best bet is to ride as fast as you can. Don't stop to talk to anyone."

"I'll never find my way," I said in despair.

"What do you mean?" Dad asked.

"Aren't the fields just a maze of small roads?"

Dad shook his head, grinning slightly. "Things have changed a bit. There's a major four-lane highway now from I-15 all the way to the foot of West Mountain. You can't miss the city."

My inner strength collapsed as I stared into the darkness. "I can't do it, Dad!"

We got off our bikes and held each other close. Dad then

began to pray. I listened as he pleaded with the Lord to protect and guide me. Then he gave me a short father's blessing. I then offered my own prayer, and my courage slowly returned.

As we got back on our bikes Dad said, "Come straight to the temple when you find the kids. Hopefully we'll see you soon." I blew him a kiss, then pedaled down 400 South into the unknown.

Within a few blocks I pedaled up the first overpass. I stopped for several moments at the top to survey the dark valley. I shuddered to see a few campfires burning between me and the huge bonfire on West Mountain. Those were likely the guards' outposts. I knew the town was nearly 10 miles away, and I was already exhausted. But a gruff voice from behind me gave me all the adrenaline I needed to press forward. "Hey Cory! Is that you?"

I glanced back to see three tall figures walking up the overpass. "I think it's a girl!" one of the figures said.

"You're dreaming," another said. "No girl would come out here alone! She'd get attacked within minutes."

Upon hearing those encouraging words, I took off down the overpass and pedaled out of earshot.

• • • •

My only companion was the moon as I pedaled down the highway. As I approached the I-15 overpass, I saw a building on the south side of the road I didn't recognize. The building's sign read, "W l-Ma," which confused me until I realized a few letters had fallen off. Wal-Mart must've come to Springville after I began this latest journey through time.

A few people gathered near a small fire in the store entrance, and I realized the people at Wal-Mart were supposed to be watching the road for intruders like me. I was grateful they were doing such a poor job. I later passed a circle of tents along the road, but I was gone before the people at the campfire could even respond.

An hour later I reached a spot where the highway curved north along West Mountain's foothills. A large subdivision lay below me, and I was within half a mile of the biggest cluster of fires.

The center of town had been built on the mountain's northeastern slope where the mountain had once jutted out into Utah

Lake, but now I could see the moonlight dancing off water nearly a half-mile further away from the shoreline I'd known.

A rhythmic drumbeat reached my ears, and I instinctively slowed my speed as I focused on the campfires. I felt certain I was being watched.

Hide the bike. The prompting was gentle and I nearly ignored it. But then I slowed to a stop and walked the bike to a nearby bush. I wedged it tightly between the limbs and returned to gaze at the bonfires. I was close enough to see people dancing around the flames.

A faint rustling came from behind the bush and I swirled around, searching the darkness. I thought I heard a whisper, and I nervously backed away. "Is somebody there?"

A young woman's voice softly asked, "What brought you here? If you're here out of curiosity, leave while you still can."

"I didn't want to get near this place, but I'm looking for someone—two people, actually. A boy and a girl."

The bush rustled again and a thin, blonde girl wearing a black dress stepped into view. "I think I can help you."

Chapter Fifteen

The girl approached me slowly. "Don't be frightened," she said quietly. "My name is Tara, and if you stick with me you'll be safe."

"How can I trust you?" I asked, backing away even further. Tara looked about 16 and rather harmless, but I had to be cautious. "Is this a trap?"

Tara stopped. "I have actually saved you from something worse."

She pulled out what appeared to be night-vision goggles and told me to put them on. "Look ahead about a hundred yards," Tara said.

I scanned the hillside and was startled to see six men on a small plateau a few feet from the road. They were joking around and wrestling.

"They can't see us because of the flames, but if you'd passed them, you would've been in real trouble," Tara said. "As I said before, I'm only here to help you."

I now trusted Tara, knowing she'd saved me from being attacked. "What are you doing out here?" I asked. "Do you do this every night?"

Tara began to answer, but then she stiffened. She took the goggles from me and scanned the road behind us. "Oh great! Here comes a group that's even more dreadful. Let's get out of here."

She grabbed my hand and led me across the road and up a rocky hillside. Someone shouted at us, but Tara kept guiding me upward. Within a quarter-mile we reached a paved road. "Once we get to the hideout I'll answer your questions, but it isn't safe out here tonight. Tomorrow is another Sacrifice Day, and Mo's party seems to be starting early."

• • • •

We followed the road to a cul-de-sac high on the mountain

where four large houses had been built. All four looked vacant, but Tara led me to the front door of the smallest home, where she gave a strange slow-paced knock.

We heard some locks being unlatched, then a purple-haired girl cautiously opened the door. She greeted Tara, then she gave me a surprised smile. "Hello there," she said. "I'm Devri, and welcome to our hideout. You'll be safe here."

I followed Tara inside the candle-lit room and saw six teenage girls sitting on worn-out couches. They all looked curiously at my—Mary's—dress. "Where did you find such a nice dress?" one of them asked.

"My mom gave it to me," I said.

That prompted a flurry of questions from the girls. "Your mom is still alive? How did you get past the guards? Why did you come here?"

Tara asked them to quiet down, then she said, "First, please introduce yourself."

I somehow remembered to use my old nickname. "My name is Eddie. I'm here to find two teenagers and take them back to Provo."

The group chuckled. "Eddie, people can't just leave here," Tara said. "These people either brainwash you into their way of life, or they eventually sacrifice you. I tried to escape once, but I didn't make it very far. The guards tried to beat such ideas out of me, and they nearly killed me."

She paused to raise her shirt high enough to show us deep scars across her back. "I pretended to conform, then I slipped into hiding," she said. "I decided if I couldn't escape, I'd at least be on the lookout for newly arrived girls, hoping to help them avoid what I did. That's why I helped start this hideout."

"That's very courageous," I said admiringly.

"She's had a busy week," said a girl who was standing against the wall. "She saved me yesterday after my brother abandoned me. I wouldn't have lasted the night."

I looked closely at the tall, brown-haired girl. "Are you Heather Dalton?" I asked.

The girl's mouth fell open. "Yes, I am. How did you know?"

"Your grandparents asked me to help you return home," I said with a sad smile. "It looks like we've got our work cut out for us."

. . . .

I removed my backpack and shared the food Dad had prepared for me. The girls acted as if I'd brought them a seven-course meal.

As we ate, Tara introduced me again to Devri, the happy, purple-haired girl who had opened the door. "Devri was the only nice person I met here after my escape attempt," Tara said. "We've worked together since that day to create this hideout. I trust her with my life."

Devri smiled kindly and then pointed to her hair. "You're wondering about it, aren't you?"

I shrugged. "It *is* an interesting color."

"It's part of my disguise," she said. "I change my hair color every few days so I won't look familiar to anyone when it's my turn to go out searching for new arrivals."

"That makes sense," I said. "How many girls have you helped over the years?"

Devri counted on her fingers. "About nine a year," she said. "Each winter we'd plan an escape during a big snowstorm, and that worked well because the guards weren't eager to leave their camp-fires. But it hasn't snowed for two years, and there haven't been as many newcomers, either. So we're down to just the six of us here now. All the other girls in town have pretty much been converted to Mo's wicked ways."

There were many more questions I wanted to ask them, but it was well past midnight. Besides, everyone was extremely tired after our meal. Tara gave me some blankets and I snuggled up on the floor, where I promptly fell asleep after my exhausting night.

When I woke up the next morning I could hear voices coming from upstairs. I soon joined the other girls at the kitchen table, where they were eating a breakfast of tomatoes, radishes and carrots. Tara offered me some, and I bit into a half-ripened tomato.

Heather came to my side. "Good morning, Eddie. Did you sleep well?"

"Better than I thought I would. How about you?"

"Actually, I stayed awake trying to figure out who you are. Where did you see my grandparents?"

"At the temple. I've been close to your family for a long

time, and my only goal is to get you and Justin safely back to the temple."

Heather's brow furrowed. "Don't even mention my brother! He got me into this mess, and I hope I never see him again!"

I was surprised at the depth of her anger. "What did he do to you?"

Heather frowned and gritted her teeth. "He tricked me into coming here, and then as soon as we got to Lincoln Point, he went straight to a big building that had evil-looking people hanging around outside. He wanted me to go in with him, but I wouldn't, so he left me there in the street. He didn't even look back at me! Some of the men outside gave me filthy stares and began walking toward me when Tara grabbed my arm and whisked me away."

Tara had been listening to our conversation. "I saw Justin and Heather come into town, and I immediately knew Heather didn't belong here. I reached her at the first possible opportunity."

"Thank you so much," Heather said, giving Tara a grateful hug. "You saved me from a horrible experience."

As we talked, I could sense that Heather was still worried about Justin, despite her anger at him. So I carefully probed her true feelings. "Heather, I understand how you feel, but shouldn't we help Justin before he gets in too deep? I don't want him to lose his soul."

Heather's jaw muscles tightened, but my words had hit home. "You're right," she said. "But isn't it already too late? There's no way to find him without actually going down there."

"We have a way," Tara said. "Our chances aren't good, but there's still hope. Follow me."

Tara led us to a top-floor bedroom. At the window was a three-foot long telescope. "This is where we take shifts looking for new arrivals," Tara said.

I stepped to the window and looked out over Lincoln Point. The city was actually smaller than I'd thought. There were maybe 800 houses, along with some city offices. Halfway down the slope was the park and community swimming pool Dad had mentioned. I couldn't see the pool itself, but a high dive rose above a fenced-off area. I could see people mingling around the smoldering bonfires.

"Like I said, the odds are slim we'll find him, but let's give it a try," Tara said. "Heather, why don't you keep the telescope trained on the downtown area? I rescued you in front of Mo's

Palace." Tara pointed to a building I figured had once been City Hall. "I'll bet that's where Justin is."

Heather adjusted the telescope and began her search, while I grabbed Tara by the arm. "Who is Mo? He's been mentioned a couple of times."

Tara smiled. "Mo is our nickname for The Mighty One, the egotistical ruler of this city. He's a disgusting person and doesn't deserve a proper title, so I just call him Mo. No one knows his real name."

She patted Heather on the shoulder. "Give a shout if you see your brother," she said. "I'm going to show Eddie around the house."

We returned to the kitchen and I looked out the back window. The back yard had been turned into a large garden, and I could see Devri and another girl picking tomatoes. The yard was completely surrounded by huge piles of trash, which Tara said served to hide the garden from outsiders.

I saw an outhouse in the far corner, which reminded me of a very urgent matter, and I excused myself. I easily remembered my first trip into an outhouse—at Bishop Aaron Johnson's home in 1868 Springville. I now entered another outhouse more than 150 years later and could only chuckle as I spied a few faded copies of *The Deseret News* piled next to the seat for use as toilet paper. It felt like I'd come full-circle.

· · · ·

Just before noon we heard an excited shout come from the top floor. Tara and I rushed to Heather, who had the telescope trained on an area near City Hall.

"It's Justin, all right," Heather said. "I suspected it was him a while ago, but I've just been waiting for him to roll over."

Heather offered me the telescope, and I looked through it to see a boy lying on the sidewalk. He was struggling to sit up, but he kept toppling over.

"That's Justin?" I asked. "He looks drunk."

"I'm sure he is," Tara said. "If you don't drink Mo's fermented brew, you aren't accepted. It looks like Justin made sure he fit in."

I turned away from the telescope. "He's in no condition for

a rescue."

"Maybe he won't even want to come with us," Heather said coldly.

Tara shook her head. "Once that hangover really sets in, it'll be the perfect time to convince him to leave Lincoln Point's party scene. Keep an eye on him, and we'll try to rescue him tonight. If we can get him back here, maybe we'll be able to talk some sense into him."

Justin hardly moved all day, and by evening we'd made plans for Tara, Heather and I to bring him back to the hideout, even if we had to drag him. As the sun set, we began a slow walk toward town. I trembled in anticipation and fear. Tara said we'd likely be left alone if we just acted casual. We each picked up a discarded drink container to appear as part of the "in crowd."

We reached Justin, who was sitting in a daze on the steps of City Hall just a few yards from the rekindled bonfire. "That must've been quite a mixture he drank," I whispered to Tara.

"I think he just overdid it," she whispered back.

We cautiously approached him, and Heather sat down next to him. "Hello, big brother. It's me, Heather. How are you feeling?"

Justin gave her a strange look but said nothing, so Heather said, "These two women want to help us get back to Provo. Come with us."

To our surprise Justin stood on his feet and shouted, "I'm not going anywhere! I like it here! You can go back to Provo if you want!" Then he collapsed to the ground, and several people turned to look at us.

"Let's get out of here," Tara said quietly. We started walking back up the hill. It was nearly dark, and if we could get away from the light of the bonfire we'd be all right.

"Stop those girls," someone shouted, and suddenly it was too late. Tara and Heather sprinted away, but I caught my foot on the hem of my antique dress. I tumbled to the road and curled up in terror.

"At least we got one of them," a man said. I was quickly yanked to my feet by several young men with goatees, who pinned my arms behind my back.

"How old do you think she is?" one of them asked. "She might be over the age limit. Should we go ahead and kill her?"

"I'm 22," I said hastily.

The men hesitated, then a raspy-voiced man said, "Maybe she's lying, but who cares? We've caught us a fine-looking female. The Mighty One might like her, and he'll reward us well."

Joyful, masculine shouts drowned out my screams as I was lifted off the ground. A canvas bag was placed over my head before I could even blink. I kicked and thrashed around, but there were too many of them holding me tight. "Hold still," the raspy voice ordered. "If you move another muscle, we'll cut your head off." That got my attention.

I could feel myself being carried down the road, and I nearly fainted when the apparent leader said, "If the Mighty One rejects her, we'll see if Sammy is hungry again."

I was carried up some steps, and I assumed we were back at City Hall. "Tell the Mighty One we've found a treasure for him," the leader called out. The men dropped my feet, but they didn't release my arms.

It was frustrating to not be allowed to see, speak or move. All I could do was listen intently. A trumpet blared loudly, and I was pushed down into a kneeling position with my head bowed as my captors also dropped to their knees.

"Oh Mighty One. Oh Mighty One," the people began to chant reverently, and I sensed a path being cleared for someone to stand in front of me. "Remove the hood," a voice ordered, and the bag was quickly taken from my head.

I slowly moved my eyes upward to see who stood before me, and in a million years I never could've predicted the Mighty One's appearance.

It was almost laughable.

Chapter Sixteen

As I raised my eyes to the Mighty One, I first saw a pair of unlaced Nike football cleats on his feet—with no socks. He wasn't wearing pants — just a small cloth that barely covered his...loins. From the waist up the Mighty One wore an old-style royal blue BYU football uniform, including shoulder pads, with a BYU football helmet on his head.

I involuntarily gasped, and the man smiled, taking my gasp as a sign of intimidation. In reality, I was just astonished that anyone would go out in public that way. I peered through the face mask at a man in his late-20s—at least. He might've been 30. His red hair hung below the helmet and flowed down over the shoulder pads, but unlike the other men, he was clean-shaven. The No. 8 was firmly planted on his chest.

I'd seen enough and finally laughed out loud, flustering the Mighty One. "How dare you laugh at me?" he asked.

"Could you please turn around for a moment?" I asked the Mighty One—or Mo, as Tara called him. He was so surprised at my request that he actually obeyed me. Sure enough, the name "Young" was pasted along the top of the uniform's back. Mo quickly turned around again and shouted in my face, "Bow to the Mighty One!"

Instead I asked, "Can't I just call you Mo? And where are your pants?" The crowd gasped in astonishment at my words.

"You mouthy fool," Mo muttered. He stepped forward and jerked me to my feet. "What's so funny?" he demanded.

I didn't answer, and he gave me a sinister look. "Speak, or I'll order your death!"

He bumped his shoulder pads against me in a challenging manner as the crowd erupted into a flurry of whispers. I backed up two steps and quietly asked, "Does Steve Young know you're wearing his college uniform?" Mo narrowed his eyes, but he didn't respond.

"You know who I mean? The star quarterback?" I asked.

"The two-time NFL MVP?"

Mo just grew angrier. "This woman speaks only gibberish," he shouted to the crowd. "She brings a plague among us. Let's put an end to this!"

The crowd surged forward, and the men again restrained my arms. Suddenly my wisecracks didn't seem so hilarious. As his followers crowded around us, Mo pressed his face mask into my cheek. "You should've shown respect," he whispered darkly.

"You aren't very mighty if I got under your skin that easily," I said nervously.

Mo just snorted. "What arrogance you show before the Mighty One," he said. "That's too bad, because I wouldn't mind a new feisty girl among my maidens. Sammy will like you, though."

He swiftly swung a fist into my stomach, leaving me doubled over in pain and struggling for breath. Then he backed up and shouted, "Everyone gather at the pit!"

The crowd exploded with excitement, and I was swept off my feet again and carried up the mountain. We approached a fenced area that was topped with barbed wire. I was carried through a gate where a faded metal sign read, *Lincoln Point Community Pool.* Mo was already inside, standing atop the high dive, which was colorfully painted as if it were a sacred tower.

"Replace the hood," he shouted to my captors. "We don't want to give Big Mouth any hints at what's coming." The crowd laughed loudly at his nickname for me, and I took my first good look at this group just before the hood was put over my head. No one in the crowd was older than 25, and most were teenagers. There were several small children running around naked—surely the group's unfortunate offspring.

My captors put me on my feet and pushed me forward a few yards before stopping. "Thank you, my faithful guards," Mo called out. "You'll be rewarded with the maiden of your choice for this capture. Begin the ceremony."

Suddenly the guards shoved me off a ledge, and I fell several feet before landing roughly on a concrete floor. I caught myself with my hands just before hitting my head.

I staggered to my feet and ripped off the hood as Mo shouted, "Light the torches! Let Big Mouth see her destiny!"

I quickly realized I was in the deep end of the empty swimming pool. The crowd grew strangely silent, and I noticed a guard unlatch a lid at the pool's shallow end before sprinting to the fence gate and slamming it behind him. Within moments something dark seemed to be filling the shallow end. The crowd saw the movement too, and everyone went bananas. They began chanting, "Sammy! Sammy! Sammy!"

I shuddered as the torches illuminated my approaching opponent—the thickest, longest snake I'd ever seen.

Chapter Seventeen

The snake's massive body curved and glided from one side of the empty pool to the other, blocking an easy escape. Sammy had obviously been through this many times before. I frantically looked for a pool ladder, but they'd all been removed. Mo let out a hoot from the high dive. "Sorry to bet against you, Big Mouth, but Sammy has never skipped a meal."

I returned my attention to the snake, which had now doubled back on itself, creating an imposing barrier across the shallow end of the pool. The monster was at least 40 feet long.

I quickly saw the snake's plan, which had surely succeeded dozens of times previously. Sammy wanted me to try a panicked escape across him, where he'd squeeze me like a tube of toothpaste as soon as I got within five feet of him.

The crowd was getting restless, and they started shouting obscenities. A few pieces of garbage were thrown at me. Apparently these "feedings" usually didn't take long.

"Come on, just jump across him," Mo shouted down at me. "We'll set you free if you get out of the pool. Impress the crowd!"

Patience, a voice whispered. *Go to the corner and be still.*

I was surprised to feel the prompting amid all the commotion, but I slowly moved to the darkest corner of the pool. I could see the snake's massive head moving back and forth. It had to be some sort of mutated python. Its tongue flicked the air, trying to locate me, but all the noise had distracted him. Sammy couldn't pinpoint my location.

The crowd soon got bored with my tactic. Many people left as the waiting game dragged on, but dozens stayed glued to the fence. Then I spotted a familiar face. Justin! He was crouched against the fence, watching the snake with a shocked expression. At that moment a fistfight broke out among some men behind him, and Justin was pushed against the fence. He shouted in pain and turned around, only to be punched in the face. Then he got swallowed up in the crowd as the fight blossomed.

I was worried about Justin, but I had my own troubles to deal with as Sammy finally began slithering in my direction. My mind went numb for a moment, but as I scampered to the opposite corner an idea popped into my head. I quickly pulled off Mary's dress and wrapped it around my right fist. I glanced up to locate the snake just as a shadow passed over me.

Wham! The snake's massive midsection smacked against my shoulder and knocked me against the wall. Whoa! If that coiled body had gone just a little higher I'd have been lassoed and crushed.

Mo let out a whoop from above. "He almost wrapped you up on the first try! One more time, Sammy!"

I watched in horror as that mid-section again curved through the air at me. I darted to the side, but the snake's tail coiled around my ankle. The snake brought its head toward me and snapped its jaws.

"Whoo-hoo! You've got him mad!" the pantless fool shouted. "Sammy always goes for the squeeze first, but it looks like he wants to swallow you alive!"

The snake's head moved dangerously close, and I stumbled backward. The snake didn't hesitate, and its jaws shot open like lightning.

But I was ready.

I held the wadded-up dress before me, and the snake swallowed it up to my elbow. I yanked my arm free and the snake halted briefly, surprised by my tactic. So I wrapped my arms around Sammy's jaws and held on tightly.

My life is over, I thought.

Sammy went wild, slamming me to the pool floor as he tried to jerk his head free. The snake was incredibly strong, and if he slammed me hard enough, he'd crack me open like a walnut.

Sammy dragged me across the pool bottom, and I somehow wrapped my legs behind his skull while still holding those dangerous jaws shut. Sammy lifted me off the ground and slammed me into a wall, but luckily his snout hit first, lessening the brunt of the collision. I could tell he'd hurt himself.

Sammy and I were now face-to-face, and I sensed this creature's only goal was to eat me. Sammy next tried to squeeze me to death, but curiously he wasn't able to coil around me without coiling his own head. Twice he got me in a pretty good grip with his midsection, but he soon relaxed, rather than squeeze his own skull.

The crowd's fistfight had turned into a noisy, full-scale brawl, but the small portion of the crowd that was still watching me shouted with glee every time Sammy seemed to have me in a death grip.

I was so weak I could hardly hold his jaws shut any longer. Then Sammy changed tactics and rhythmically pounded me from side to side. I felt like a bucking bronc-rider with a foot stuck in the stirrup. My shoulders and hips were getting bruised, and there was no doubt Sammy would eventually win the battle. I just closed my eyes and maintained my grip as the frustrated snake tried to shake me off.

"Guards, corral Sammy!" I heard Mo shout, followed by a rush of footsteps. I opened my eyes to see two dozen men jumping into the pool. They each grabbed the snake at two-foot intervals, and Mo followed them with a thick forked stick. He pushed the stick down against Sammy's neck and shouted to me, "Get away! I've got him!"

I rolled away and staggered out of the pool. The brawl stopped instantaneously—the crowd had never seen anyone leave Sammy's pit alive. As I approached the gate, the crowd greeted me with cheers and pats on the back. Someone with a gash over his eye offered me a cup of brownish brew, but I pushed it away.

I tried to spot Justin in the crowd, but he was likely lying in a pool of blood. I headed to where I'd last seen him, but Mo shouted, "Take her to the palace! Let's honor our new queen!"

The crowd eagerly responded to their leader's announcement, and I was lifted off the ground and carried down the hill to City Hall.

Ugh! The Mighty One's queen? I could only shudder. I'd already fought off one serpent.

Chapter Eighteen

I was carried into what must've once been Lincoln Point's city council room. The room was well-lit by torches, and right in the middle of the room was a huge mattress, surrounded by folding chairs. Its purpose was horribly obvious.

Mo's followers put me down and I wearily sat on a chair as well-wishers crammed into the room. "No one's ever beaten Sammy," a long-haired, shirtless guy said to me. "You're stupendously gnarly." I still can't decide if that was a compliment.

Within seconds Mo made his grand entrance. Everyone bowed to him except me, but he didn't seem bothered by my lack of respect for him. He stood before me and held out his hand. "I must ask your name," he said.

"It's Eddie," I said, sticking with my nickname.

"Eddie?" Mo asked in surprise. "That's an unusual name for a girl, but your performance against Sammy was also unusual. I can't wait to see you demonstrate those skills with me on the mattress."

The crowd let out whoops and hollers as if we were on a sleazy daytime talk show. I stayed silent, but I vowed to fight tooth and nail before I'd snuggle up to that savage. I still needed to find Justin, though, so I took advantage of the group's new respect for me.

"Could you please answer a question, Mighty One?" I asked.

"With pleasure," Mo said as he removed his helmet and ran his fingers through his red mane of hair. He moved to the bed and stretched out on it. It wasn't a pretty sight.

"What does the symbol on your helmet stand for?" I asked.

Mo grinned. "As my followers know, it represents the power of a past civilization. You can still see their great forked monument on Wa Mountain."

My ears perked up. "What did you say? Wa Mountain?"

"Yes. I barely remember the days before the war, and it has

always been known as Wa Mountain," Mo said. I smiled inside, witnessing the effects of someone's lazy pronunciation on a young boy's mind.

"So that's where you got your armor, right?" I asked.

Mo nodded. "One night many years ago my warriors and I went to the great city at the base of Wa Mountain. We went to the huge outdoor stadium that has tall grass growing in the center. We came face-to-face with the gigantic cat that guards the entrance, but we outran him and found another way in."

Congratulations, Mo, I thought. *Only the world's greatest warriors would be able to outrun the statue in front of Cougar Stadium.*

Mo peered around the room, and he had his audience captivated. "That's where we found the secret chamber filled with this special armor. The armor I'm wearing was in a glass case, so I knew it was sacred," Mo said reverently. "Now when we raid the towns, we wear our armor and have never been defeated."

Wouldn't BYU be proud.

I stifled a laugh and asked, "What about Sammy? Where did he come from?"

"We also found him in the great city. There's a building there filled with dead animals," Mo said. "Sammy was there, inside a glass box. He was the only living thing in there, so I felt we should keep him."

"You were in the Bean Museum," I said without thinking.

"What?"

"That's the name of the building."

"I don't know that name," Mo said with a shrug. "Anyway, we brought him back with us, and for some reason 'Sammy the Snake' sounded like a good name."

He barely remembers Sesame Street, I thought sadly as I realized what Mo's generation had missed and suffered through. I found myself sympathizing with these people, despite their savage ways.

My sympathy quickly departed, though, as Mo's eyes roamed up and down my body. "I like your outfit," he said, referring to my jeans and sweater. "You look much better without that dress."

Anger welled up in me, but I kept my face passive. "I see what you have in mind, Mighty One, but is there somewhere I could first change out of my clothes?"

Mo nodded and pointed to a side room. "Right in there," he said eagerly. I walked toward the room and calmly said, "I'll only be a few moments."

The crowd hooted, and Mo grinned widely. I cringed inside, disgusted at what I'd hinted at, but I saw no other options for escape. I closed the door and scanned the room. The only exit was a hinged window.

Someone knocked on the door, and I quickly stuck my head out. "I'll be right with you, Mighty One," I said sweetly to Mo. The crowd cheered loudly as I hastily closed the door again. I found a folding chair and jammed it under the doorknob.

I went to the window and saw that only the window's bottom portion opened. It swung into the room like a hinge and would be a tight squeeze. The plump Emma I'd seen in the photo never would've made it, but I was still skinny enough to make it through.

I climbed onto the sill and carefully inched my way through the window, but I soon became wedged. However, another knock on the door was all the motivation I needed to quickly wiggle outside.

I sneaked away from the building and ran back toward Sammy's pit. I wasn't sure if Justin was still there, but I felt I had to give him one more chance, whether he deserved it or not. A knife was lying along the road and I picked it up, figuring it might come in handy.

A few torches still flickered around the pool, and I was able to find Justin laying on a picnic table near the fence. His face was bloody, and he kept rubbing his right thigh as he moaned softly.

I heard a loud crash come from City Hall, and I knew Mo's followers had broken down the door I'd wedged shut. Within moments the streets would be swarming with young people eager to kill me.

"Justin, get up," I said urgently. My voice startled him, and he fearfully looked up at me. "You're the Snake Woman," he gasped. "Leave me alone!" He tried to roll away, but I flashed the knife in his face.

"Keep quiet!" I ordered. "We're getting out of here."

He cautiously climbed off the table, and I put the knife against his ribs while clutching the back of his shirt with my other hand. I pushed him toward the road and headed to Tara's hideout. I quickened my pace, knowing a reunion with Sammy—or worse, with Mo—awaited me if I got caught.

Chapter Nineteen

A glance down the hillside showed an army of torch-bearing thugs were spreading out from City Hall. "They'll soon have the city covered," I said. "Let's hope I can remember the right house."

"Where are you taking me?" Justin asked nervously.

"Just be quiet," I said, still tempted to leave him. "It was your selfish ways that brought me here in the first place."

"Do I even know you?" Justin whined. My only response was a slight knife poke between his ribs.

The full moon was now shining brightly. It had to be nearly midnight. I was tiring fast, but we climbed the hill and within minutes I saw Tara's hideout at the end of the cul-de-sac. "That's it," I said excitedly.

We went up to the door and I tried to imitate the knock Tara had given. I failed terribly, but within seconds I saw a curtain move. "Hey, it's me, Eddie," I called out softly. Soon Tara opened the door and pulled us inside.

"I escaped from Mo, and I found Heather's brother," I said as Justin slumped to the floor and stared silently at us.

"Good job," she said. "I was going to try rescuing you, but it looks like you can take care of yourself."

I quickly told Tara how I escaped from City Hall, and her expression grew grim. "You have to leave immediately," she said.

"Can't we just rest?" I asked. "I'm very tired."

Tara shook her head. "We saw them take you to the snake pit, and I watched Mo through the telescope. As you battled the snake, Mo's expression changed from glee to genuine concern for you—an emotion I've never seen in him. I'm afraid he might actually like you, which isn't good. It means you must either become his queen or get as far away as possible, because he'll search everywhere for you."

"Then I'm getting out of here," I said.

"Good choice. I'll get Heather, then we can go."

"Are you coming with us?" I asked.

"Yes," she said firmly. "I've often told the other girls a day might come when I'd try to find my parents. I feel now is the time. Devri is willing to stay here and continue what we started."

Tara climbed the stairs and soon returned with Heather, who stopped short at the sight of her brother. "Justin! How did you get here?"

He pointed at me. "Snake Woman forced me to come with her."

Heather got right in his face. "How could you leave me like that? If Tara hadn't helped me, I'd probably be dead! What do you have to say?"

Justin bowed his head. "I just...well, I wanted to see what it's like here. But I hate it—I got the tar beat out of me. Please forgive me."

Heather wasn't finished fuming, but she finally turned toward the back door. "Come on. Let's get out of here."

Justin promised to cooperate if I'd keep the knife out of his back. I believed him only because he looked pretty thrashed from the fight. He was in no condition to outrun us. We climbed through a small opening in the trash pile and started up the rocky slope—and just in time. A few torch-bearers were within a hundred yards of the house.

"What about the other girls?" I asked Tara.

"They're already safe," she said. "We have a small camper buried in the trash pile that we hide in when Mo's followers approach the house. And Devri is actually out on her shift. She's downtown right now looking for other girls to save."

"She seems so fearless," I said.

Tara nodded. "The hideout is in good hands."

There weren't any houses higher on the hill, and we scrambled through sage brush. The steep mountainside was covered with loose rocks, and I could feel thick cobwebs crossing between all the bushes. I shuddered and hoped the spiders were sleeping.

The torches now filled the entire city below us. It wouldn't take Mo's henchmen very long to realize we weren't there. We were outnumbered, so we'd have to outwit them.

• • • •

Within 20 minutes we reached a dirt road that curved upward along the hillside. We didn't want to go any higher on the barren mountain, but there were still some torch-bearers coming in our direction. We seemed trapped, but then an idea came to my mind. "We've got to get to the tower," I told the others.

"You mean the big one on top of the mountain?" Tara asked. "What good would that do?"

I pointed down at the town. "See the torches? Most of them are searching the lake shore and along the foothills. I'm sure this group below us will turn back soon. I feel if we reach the tower we'll be safe, partly because we'll be able to see anyone coming."

The others didn't have a better idea, so we continued our march up the mountain. It took us another three hours to reach the communication tower, which stood darkly above us. There were also a few smaller towers, but I felt compelled to stay near the biggest one.

A chainlink fence had once surrounded the tower, but vandals had cut a large hole in it. We entered the enclosure as the first hints of dawn emerged, and I collapsed against one of the tower's footings.

"Let's enjoy the sunrise," I said. The others acted as if they'd never heard of such a concept, but the girls soon joined me. Justin stayed close by, but he hadn't spoken since we left the house. Hopefully, Heather's words had pricked his conscience.

We silently watched the valley below, then we squinted as the first slice of the sun suddenly peeked over Maple Mountain to the east of us. "Oh, it's so bright," Tara said.

As the valley filled with light, I was surprised to see all the hay fields that once separated Springville, Spanish Fork, and Payson were now filled with homes and businesses, creating a solid band of buildings from I-15 to the mountains.

I didn't see any movement in the cities, though. There wasn't even a light on. It was an eerie scene. I remembered how busy these cities had once been. I could see the light towers at Payson High School's football field, and I realized these teenagers had never even seen a prep football game.

I began to feel depressed as I realized how quickly my companions had been forced to grow up. Tara had mentioned she was nearly 17, and she'd already been running a women's shelter for three years. And at age 13, Heather seemed much more grown-up than most 18-year-olds I'd known.

As for Justin, so far he'd acted like a typical, worldly 15-year-old boy. But maybe his decisions would've been different if he'd ever had the chance to attend a church youth activity or play miniature golf with good friends. Instead, he was running for his life.

Finally Heather nudged me. "Eddie, are you OK?"

"Oh, sorry. I was just remembering happier times," I said. "Well, do you have any ideas on how we can get back to the temple?"

Heather's eyes brightened. "You're taking us back to the temple? Oh, how wonderful! I never thought I'd see my grandparents again."

Justin came closer and narrowed his eyes at me. "There's something very strange about you." He turned to the girls. "Do you know what Eddie did last night? She wrestled a gigantic snake into submission."

Tara nodded. "It's pretty amazing. It's never been done before." She put her hand on my shoulder. "How did you survive?"

"Plain luck, plus Heavenly Father's help."

Tara seemed troubled, as if I'd triggered a distant memory. "You guys are different from everyone else in Lincoln Point," she said. "I've never heard any of them mention Heavenly Father."

I sensed Tara had seen many tragedies in her life. "What made you come to Lincoln Point?" I asked her quietly.

She sighed. "I'd always heard that Lincoln Point was where all the fun was, so I slipped away with Mo's guards when they came through Provo a few years ago. I was only 12 years old. What a mistake!"

"Didn't you miss your family?" I asked.

"Not at first," Tara said. "My parents were planning to go to a place called New Jerusalem, and I was scared to leave. The guards made Lincoln Point sound so great, and it was fun at first. I tried their potions and drinks, and they accepted me. But I'd lose control and do things I now regret. I tried to escape once, but I paid for it."

She lifted the back of her shirt to show Justin the scars she'd showed us earlier, and he seemed greatly bothered by them. "The Mighty One's guards did that to you?" he asked.

She gave him an exasperated look. "Those people are evil!

They tried to feed Eddie to a snake! Don't you get it?"

Justin mumbled something under his breath and moved to the other side of the tower compound. I placed my arm around Tara's shoulders and said, "I have some good news for you. I know where New Jerusalem is."

Heather spoke up. "I do too!"

Tara's eyes sparkled. "Really? Is it far?"

"It's pretty far," Heather said. "My Dad's sister Emma lives there, though. I'm sure she'll help us find your parents."

"That's wonderful," Tara said through tears. "I miss them so much."

I pulled Tara to me and she cuddled against my shoulder, where I held her for a long time and stroked her hair. "You're a courageous person," I whispered in her ear. "We'll help you find your family."

Chapter Twenty

Justin eventually walked over to the edge of the road and watched below for Mo's warriors. A steady breeze blew across the mountaintop, and it had lulled the rest of us to sleep, but we jerked awake upon hearing Justin's hurried footsteps.

"Hey, we're in trouble," Justin said urgently. "The same guys that beat me up are climbing the hill!"

We were trapped! They'd surely discover us if we hid in the small cinderblock building at the base of the tower, and we didn't dare scramble down the steep face of the mountain. We had only one way to go. Up.

"Follow me," I said. We scrambled around to the far side of the tower and began scaling the cross beams. Fifteen feet above the ground we reached a metal ladder that led to the red signal light at the very top of the tower. The light had once been used to alert airplanes, but now it was just another relic of days gone by.

I hastily climbed the ladder and was soon alongside a wooden platform at the tower's highest level. Getting onto the platform would require letting go of the ladder, which seemed risky as a powerful gust of wind rocked the tower. The others were behind me on the ladder, and we were at least 150 feet above the mountaintop. The mountain's eastern slope dropped away rapidly, making it seem we were several thousand feet in the air.

My knees were shaking, but I finally let go of the ladder and grabbed onto the platform. The wind tried to pull me off the tower, but I slipped my fingers into a hole in the wood and pulled myself to safety.

Heather came next, and she nearly didn't make it. My heart pounded as her fingers searched furiously for the hole in the wood. She finally found it, and I grabbed her arm and pulled her next to me. Tara and Justin had difficulties too, but soon we were all on the platform. The height made me feel dizzy and I lay on my back, while Tara and Heather sat down and clung to each other. Only Justin seemed unfazed as he leaned over the edge and reported that the band of teenagers had reached the top of the hill and were moving toward the tower. "Lie flat, or we're dead," I said.

The hole in the wood was actually a two-inch gap in the middle of the platform, and Justin put his face against it. "Those guys are still hanging around," he whispered nervously. "I don't think they'd come up here, though."

"The Mighty One will search everywhere for Eddie," Tara said softly. "One of his maidens tried to escape once, and he chased her all the way to Salt Lake." She looked at me. "Just imagine the effort he'll make to recapture his queen!"

Ping! A pebble ricocheted off the red bulb above us. "They've got sling-shots!" Justin said anxiously. A few more rocks pinged off the tower, then the assault stopped.

"Maybe they're leaving," Heather said hopefully.

Justin shook his head. "One of them is climbing up here!"

We sat in numb silence and listened to a guy work his way up the rickety metal ladder. A powerful gust of wind struck him, and he let out a string of profanities. His buddies below laughed at him.

"You come up here!" he shouted down at them. We could hear him mutter to himself as the wind howled around him. "No one's hiding up here!" he shouted again. "I'm coming down!"

We breathed a sigh of relief, but then someone shouted, "Look on the platform, maggothead!"

We all watched the top of the ladder in fear, knowing our lives were over if Maggothead saw us. His hands appeared, and then his face.

"Hello," I said calmly.

"Hey," he said in surprise. "How..."

Swoosh! A monstrous burst of wind rattled the tower, and Maggothead took the brunt of it. He was gone! We could barely hear his screams over the wind. Justin peered again through the gap in the platform. "The whole group's moving to the other side of the tower," he reported. "I don't see the guy."

Then he recoiled. "Oh, there he is. What a mess."

Of course, we all had to take a look. The mangled body was embedded in the gravel below us, and the hoodlums were gathered around their dead friend. It disturbed me that some of the boys were laughing about it. Eventually they piled some gravel over the body and headed back to the city.

"That was gruesome, but I feel Heavenly Father saved us," Heather said. "I don't think those guys will be back."

We agreed, and I offered a prayer of thanks in my heart.

. . . .

It was barely noon, and I didn't feel safe leaving the tower yet. We agreed to wait until dark, and we tried to make ourselves comfortable on the platform.

Now that the crisis was over, Justin became more curious about me. "I don't get it," he said. "You said you're taking us back to the temple. How did you even know who we are?"

"I know your father very well," I said. "I also know you don't belong in Lincoln Point."

Heather's eyes sparkled. "Are you an angel or something?"

"Hardly," I said with a roll of my eyes. "Your grandparents asked me to find you and bring you back to the temple."

"How do you know our grandparents?" Heather asked. "I've never seen you before."

Justin nodded. "Yeah! There's something strange about you."

I shrugged and smiled. "You're not the first to say that." Then I curled up in a ball. "Let's try to get some sleep. We've got a long night ahead of us."

Chapter Twenty-One

By afternoon the unceasing wind was getting on our nerves. "I need a drink," Heather moaned. "I'm feeling weak."

She didn't look well, and I knew it was time to move. "I'll bet Mo's followers are taking long naps after last night," I said. "It might be a good time to get away."

"But we can't go anywhere near the town," Tara said. "The guards will be all over us."

I carefully stood and looked to the west. I could only see a barren valley below us. The lake had once wrapped around the mountain, but now the area was just a dry lake bed. "It'll take us longer to get back to Provo, but heading west looks the safest. They won't expect us to go that way."

The others agreed and we began our descent from the tower. It was harder to get off the platform than it'd been to get on it! We nearly lost Tara in the process. She lost her grip as she tried to get back on the ladder, but I grabbed her shirt before she fell. We all breathed a sigh of relief when we finally reached the tower's base, then we started down the west side of the mountain. I took the lead, and I saw that my worries about the cobwebs the night before were well-founded. Large spiders resided in every bush, and although they'd scurry away, it bothered me a lot. It also slowed our progress.

"Justin, please take the lead," I said. "These spiders scare me."

He grinned. "You wrestled a huge snake, but you're scared of spiders?"

"Well, yes."

He teased me a little, but then he stepped forward and used a stick to break the cobwebs. The hillside was covered with loose rocks, and Heather slipped badly once, scraping her elbows, but by sunset we'd reached the paved road that wrapped around the mountain. Our throats were parched, but I convinced them to stay on the road for a while rather than go directly to the lake. We moved along it for about a mile before seeing torches in the distance as night fell.

"OK, we can get a drink now," I said. We crossed the dry lake bed for several yards, then the ground turned soft. The mud was up to our knees before we actually reached the water. Utah Lake still had the same slimy-green look it has always been known for, but we didn't care as we scooped up handfuls of water.

Once we'd had enough to drink, Tara asked, "What now? I don't feel safe going back to the road."

"Me neither," I said. "We're too close to the city already. I think our only option is to wade to Provo."

They seemed surprised. "Come on, it's not too deep," I said. "I went water-skiing out here once and hit the bottom when I crashed. Surely we can wade across now with the water so low."

They looked at me strangely. Justin finally asked, "What's water-skiing?"

"You know...with a motorboat," I said, knowing I'd used a very bad example.

"I've never seen a boat on the lake," Tara said.

"It was a long time ago," I said hastily. "Let's get farther out into the lake."

They were still puzzled, but they followed me out into the water. We soon rounded West Mountain's northern end, and I finally saw where Mo's followers kept getting fuel for their fires. Several men were hacking apart a home along the shore and carrying the pieces toward City Hall.

We were wading in waist-deep water, and someone would've been lucky to see us, but we instinctively sank down until only our heads were above the surface. This cut down on our splashing, too.

A small orange-white dot above Provo caught our attention as it flickered to life, and we first thought the mountain had caught on fire. Then I smiled with relief.

"It's the temple!" I whispered.

The others stared in amazement. "The lights haven't been turned on in years," Heather said softly. "It's beautiful! Why would they do it now?"

"To guide us home."

Soon we'd left Lincoln Point far behind as we headed straight toward the light on the hill. "We're going to make it!"

Heather said happily.

Tara was more cautious. "The Mighty One won't give up that easily. His guards are probably stationed in every city."

I noticed campfires along the Provo shoreline. "You're right. We're not safe yet."

• • • •

At dawn we struggled onto shore near the Provo Airport. We'd gulped enough lake water to halt our thirst, but now our stomachs were all growling. Justin found a dead carp and offered to cut it up for us, but none of us were *that* hungry.

We were soaked, but the morning was heating up quickly. Our clothes soon dried, and our muddy pantlegs hardened enough that we could crumple the dirt away. We all badly needed a shower, but that was far from our minds. We walked along one of the airport's runways and entered an airplane hangar, hoping to find shelter. I saw a small jet parked inside. Its tires were flat and dust covered the windshield, but otherwise it was in good shape.

"An actual airplane! I've read about these things, but I've never seen one," Heather said. "Eddie, can you fly it?"

"I don't think this one would work," I said. "But it will serve as a good hideout."

I reached up and yanked open the cockpit door. It screeched loudly, causing a bird to flutter out of the engine compartment. Then there was silence.

"I'm exhausted," I said. "Let's try to get some sleep, then we'll try to reach the temple tonight."

"Sounds good," Heather said. "Sleeping will help me forget how hungry I am."

We climbed inside. There were eight seats, and we tilted the seats back as far as they would go. It was as comfortable as could be expected. The others dozed off quickly, but I stayed awake pondering how we'd make it across Provo. Surely Mo's guards would be everywhere. Tad and I had sometimes found it difficult getting to the temple each month, but never had the task seemed as impossible as it did this time.

Chapter Twenty-Two

By noon we'd all awakened, so we decided to get moving again. We headed north toward Center Street. I'd decided our best option was to follow the bike trail along the Provo River, where we'd be hidden by the trees along the bank and maybe find some water.

An hour later we reached the bike trail, but the river wasn't there! "I can't believe this," I said. "A big river used to run here."

I think the teenagers were starting to question my sanity. "This obviously hasn't been a river for several years," Heather said. "When were you here last?"

I shifted uncomfortably. "I remember coming here when I was young," I said. "Things have certainly changed."

We stayed hidden on the trail until 800 North, where we were excited to find an abandoned raspberry patch. We each ate several handfuls of berries, which gave us a burst of energy as we moved into the heart of the city.

I was trying to figure out the best route to the temple when I saw the tall buildings of Utah Valley Regional Medical Center looming ahead. "Is that the temple?" Tara asked.

"I'm afraid not, but it means were getting close." I guided the others across the hospital's south parking lot and to the edge of the big field east of the hospital. The field was covered with piles of silt, likely dumped there after the big flood.

Out of the corner of my eye I thought I saw something move on top of the hospital. I turned to check—and immediately froze in my tracks. There were people up there, and they were wearing football helmets!

"Don't move," I softly told the others. "The Mighty One's followers are on top of that building, but it doesn't seem like we've been spotted yet."

The others stopped and peeked over their shoulders to see for themselves.

"We're history if they see us," Tara said.

I looked frantically around, but there was literally nowhere to hide. Then Heather said, "Let's just spread out and slowly work our way to the temple. I'll lead the way."

I had second thoughts about Heather leading us. She was a pretty girl who might attract attention from the thugs atop the hospital, but I didn't see another choice.

"OK, but let's go toward the mountains now," I said. "I'll follow you. Tara, you come after me, then Justin can watch our backs."

They all nodded, and we watched tensely as Heather walked among the big sand piles in the field. I waited until she'd gone about 30 yards, then I moved forward. It felt like a horrible game of cat-and-mouse. I glanced at the top of the hospital, but the guards were chatting with each other and still hadn't noticed us. It was difficult to maintain a leisurely pace, but soon we were all walking several yards apart. Our biggest obstacle now was the silence. The town was too quiet! Provo without traffic was eerie.

Heather made it to Freedom Boulevard unnoticed. She softly called back, "I don't know which way to go!"

"Go toward Provo High School," I said.

"Where's that?"

"Those burned-out buildings ahead of you," I said. "Try that gate in the fence."

Heather yanked open a chain-link door just south of the tennis courts.

Screech!

I cringed as Mo's men halted their conversation and turned in our direction. One of them scanned the area with a pair of binoculars. All four of us stopped in our tracks and tried to blend in, but the man appeared to study each of us for a moment. Then he pointed us out to his friends.

"They've seen us," I cried. "We've got to outrun them."

We ran between the buildings of Provo High and then gathered together again at the edge of University Avenue. "How far is the temple?" Heather asked. "I've never been in this part of town."

"We still have a long way to go," I said. "We'll have to outfox them."

I said a prayer in my heart, then led the kids toward BYU.

• • • •

The strength we'd gained from our meal of berries was fading, but the fear of capture pushed us on at full speed. We sprinted across the Smith Fieldhouse parking lot and reached the stairs to the upper campus. The bushes along the stairway hadn't been pruned for years, and the branches scraped our arms and faces.

We reached the small tunnel that passed under the road, and we looked back to see if we were being followed. We gasped as seemingly the whole BYU offensive line charged toward the stairway!

We finished climbing the stairs and crossed the campus toward the Lee Library. I thought if we could get downstairs, they'd never find us. We approached the entrance to the library addition but stopped short. A chain-link fence surrounded the entrance.

"Should we climb the fence?" Justin asked.

"Hold on," I said, remembering Jason saying something about it being protected. I picked up a metal bolt that had fallen out of a nearby bench and tossed it at the fence. *Zing!* A shower of sparks flew into the air as it hit.

"It's electrified," I said. "Come this way."

I led them toward the Administration Building. I noticed the Brigham Young statue was still in place, watching over campus. "That thing's indestructible," I said to myself. We hurried around the west end of the building, then cautiously peered back. The uniformed hoodlums were now standing in front of the chain-link fence, unsure if we'd entered there or not.

One of the warriors suddenly leaped up and grabbed the top of the fence. His body jolted, and his helmet bounced away as he collapsed to the ground. His four friends looked around in fear, then one of them somehow spotted us. He pointed in our direction, and we started running again.

"They'll be merciless to us after what happened to their friend," Tara said fearfully.

"They've got to catch us first," I said.

We entered the curved white walkway that crosses the road and leads to the Marriott Center. We entered the walkway and hunched down, keeping our heads below the walkway's wall to avoid being seen. As we rounded the final curve and entered the tunnel that leads to the Marriott Center, we were surprised to see an old woman sitting there.

"Who are you?" she demanded. "This is my tunnel!"

We ignored her and sprinted toward the Marriott Center's southwest doors. We stepped through a shattered outside door just as we heard the old woman shout, "They went that way!"

I flung open a portal door and peered into the pitch-black building. "Trust me and keep quiet," I said. "Hold hands and watch your step."

I led them into the portal, but rather than going down the steps, I led them upward through the darkness to the building's top row of seats. "Get flat on your stomachs and don't even breathe," I whispered.

We positioned ourselves beneath the top row of bleacher seats, and within moments the portal doors were yanked open. One of Mo's warriors rushed into the darkness and immediately toppled down the concrete stairs. He crashed onto the railing and tumbled halfway to the bottom, screaming in terror. His helmet and shoulder pads saved him from greater injury, but he still lay motionless, moaning about a broken arm.

The three remaining warriors cautiously entered the portal opening and propped open the door to let daylight in. The setting sun reflected dimly off their helmets. "What is this place?" someone asked.

"I explored it once, and it's like a dangerous maze," a familiar voice said.

The Mighty One! He'd personally joined the search!

"Was it like Conquest?" the first voice asked.

"Sort of. To win this game the warrior had to find his way to the bottom carefully without being attacked by hidden defenders," Mo said. "Not every stairway leads to the floor. Only certain paths allowed the players to reach the bottom, where great glory awaited them. This ancient civilization was very creative."

Not as creative as Mo's imagination.

Mo finally turned his attention to the wounded warrior below him. "Brian, did you see them?"

Brian stopped whimpering. "Yes, I even wrestled with them," he lied. "But they overpowered me and pushed me down the stairs."

"Which way did they go?" Mo asked excitedly.

"I tried to stop them, but they slipped past me and made it

to the bottom."

Whew! This liar was really helping us out.

Mo lit a torch and worked his way down the stairs. "Eddie, I know you're in here," Mo called out. "Give up and we'll forget everything."

The other two warriors stopped to carry Brian the Liar to the bottom of the stairs. Mo had reached the floor and was cautiously exploring the opening where one of the basketball hoops once stood.

"It's now or never," I whispered. "Let's sneak out and run to the temple."

We quietly crept down the stairs and out the portal, but Brian noticed our shadows. "There they are!" he shouted.

We sprinted halfway around the Marriott Center concourse and exited the northeast doors, but I could hardly make my legs work. Tara was also having trouble keeping up. By the time we'd crossed the debris-filled parking lot, Mo and the two other healthy warriors were exiting the Marriott Center. They must've left Brian behind.

We could now see the temple's spire in the distance. Heather seemed to be in the best shape of the four of us, so I said, "Heather, run as fast as you can to the temple and tell them we need help. We'll try to keep up."

She nodded and sprinted away.

Chapter Twenty-Three

We veered onto a side street and I spotted the buildings of the Missionary Training Center. We scaled a fence and walked quietly between the buildings, but I wasn't sure which way to go. I'd been there only once, when Doug had begun his mission.

I could sense people watching us from the buildings, and I didn't dare venture inside any of them. I finally took a gamble and entered a building with a long hallway. We soon stood before a giant world map that filled one wall. "I know where we are now," I said. "The entrance should be this way!"

We hurried through the lobby, where a few people slept on faded couches. One man gave a startled cry, but I waved at him and he merely waved back before closing his eyes again.

We exited the building and ran to 900 East. The temple complex was now only a few hundred yards away! We angled across the formerly grassy field below the temple. It was now mostly barren, with some weeds about two feet high.

We slowed to a walk, glad there wasn't any sign of Mo or his gang. We climbed the hill past a large water tank and walked toward the sand pit where missionaries had once played volleyball. We'd nearly reached the temple's western parking lot when the weeds rustled a few feet ahead of us. Someone with a blue jersey and football helmet was hiding there. I silently pointed him out to the others just as the warrior realized he'd been spotted. He stood and shouted, "Don't move! The Mighty One desires to see you!"

I realized there weren't any other warriors around. This guy seemed to be a watchman rather than one of our pursuers. "Let's try to get past him," I whispered. "It'll be easier now than when his friends show up."

We made a break for it, and I made my way to the parking lot as the warrior chased Justin for a moment. Then he changed course and zeroed in on Tara. The warrior grabbed her by the waist, flung her into the air, then smashed her to the ground.

"You bully!" I shouted. I angrily doubled back, grabbed the

guy's face mask and yanked off his helmet. It was sad to see he was just a skinny teenager with bad acne. With his helmet off, the boy's courage disappeared and he ran down the slope.

Justin quickly joined me next to Tara's motionless body. She was on her side and blood was flowing from a gash above her right ear.

"Tara, wake up, honey," I said softly, but there wasn't a response. I met Justin's fearful gaze and said, "Hurry to the temple and let your grandpa know what happened. I'll stay here with her."

Justin hurried up the hill, and I rolled Tara onto her back. She was breathing fine, but there was still no sign of consciousness. Then I heard the shout.

"I'll give you one more chance to be my queen," Mo's voice rang out. "Otherwise, we'll kill you right here. What's it going to be?"

I whirled around and saw Mo and his two pals standing on the far side of the volleyball pit. They must've come up the sidewalk. The helmetless warrior was also with them. I slowly moved away from Tara, hoping they'd forget about her. I walked toward the center of the volleyball pit and stood silently, praying the others would return soon.

"Have you lost your voice, Big Mouth?" Mo asked with a sneer. I didn't respond, and he laughingly said, "You're the weirdest girl I've ever met."

The four of them spread out around the volleyball pit and began to surround me. "Why can't you just leave me alone?" I finally asked.

"You embarrassed me in front of my followers," Mo said. "I won't rest until you return to Lincoln Point and submit to me in front of them all."

"I don't like Lincoln Point," I said calmly, trying to stall until help could arrive from the temple. "I found it rather boring there."

"Boring?" Mo asked in surprise. "We don't have any rules to obey. You can do whatever you want! I call that fun!"

"That's not true," I said. "Don't you have a rule to kill people over age 25? I'd guess you're at least 30."

Mo was silent, but I could almost see smoke coming out of his ears. The warriors turned to watch him. "Mighty One, how old are you?" asked the helmetless one.

Mo's face turned crimson. He ignored the question and shouted, "That's it, wench! You're going to die!"

He charged forward, caught me by the leg, and dragged me toward a short fence that ran between the volleyball pit and water tank. On the other side of the fence was a 20-foot drop to the base of the tank. He ordered the warriors to join him, and they each grabbed one of my limbs. "On the count of three, let's see how far this smart-mouth can fly."

The helmetless one seemed delighted. "I'll bet we can bounce her off the side of the tank," he said eagerly.

"Probably so!" Mo said. "Good thinking!"

They rocked me back and forth, preparing to throw me face first. I struggled a bit, but I was too tired to actually get away. "One, two..."

Crack!

The helmetless warrior let go of my ankle and clutched his shoulder pads, which had been shattered by a bullet.

Crack!

Another bullet clipped the helmet of the warrior holding my other ankle, leaving a scorch mark along the side. The warrior released my ankle and quickly yanked off his helmet. "What was that?" he shouted.

The distraction allowed me to get my footing and break away from Mo and the other warrior, who were peering nervously up the hillside. I gave a joyful shout as Dad and Justin stepped from behind some bushes. Dad was holding his old .22-caliber rifle.

I hurried to them as Dad kept his attention on the warriors. He shouldn't have worried. The four warriors were already halfway down the slope, with the cowardly Mo leading the way.

Dad raised the gun to his cheek and fired another shot, which hit the ground near Mo. The "mighty warrior" leaped to the side, shrieked like a girl, then sprinted even harder. The group ran down 900 East and never looked back.

"That should scare them away," Justin said.

"Don't count on it," Dad said. "They'll be back—with reinforcements."

Chapter Twenty-Four

Within moments several temple workers were there to help carry Tara up the slope. She was now conscious but complaining of a major headache. I'd expected worse after seeing how she'd been bodyslammed.

I took Dad's arm. "Whew, I'm glad you got there in time."

"Heather arrived and told us you were in trouble," Dad said. "I grabbed my gun and met Justin at the temple gate. He showed me where to find you."

The men took us to the temple's living quarters, and we were finally able to rest. I couldn't believe it'd only been two days since I'd departed for Lincoln Point. I checked on Tara's condition and let Mom fuss over me for a minute as I thanked Heather for her life-saving run. I also praised Justin for helping Dad find me.

Then Dad motioned for me to follow him. We entered a side room and he closed the door. "Things are getting really interesting around here," he said with a grin. "I think you'll now understand why I didn't let you read your book."

I was confused. "What do you mean? Haven't we followed what my book said?"

Dad shook his head. "Tara isn't mentioned anywhere in your book. You had written that you'd faced The Mighty One and escaped the snake. You'd later found Heather cowering alongside the road after she'd tried to find Justin herself, and then the two of you had tricked Justin into following you back to Provo."

"Yes, that's a bit different than what actually happened."

"But here's the most interesting part," Dad said. "When The Mighty One's followers chased you across Provo, the two kids made it back safely, but one of the warriors hit you in the head with a rock just as you entered the temple compound. You disappeared and returned to the time you belonged in."

"Whoa! So I'm overdue?"

"Possibly, but maybe you were actually meant to stay longer," he said. He went to the drawer and pulled out his copy of the book. He flipped through the final pages and shrugged. "This copy still has that original ending, but somehow everything was altered when Tara entered the picture. I have no idea what happens now. Read through the book and see if you can figure out what happened."

He handed me the book, which was titled "Escape to Provo." I carefully read the book late into the night, and just as I was dozing off, a seemingly small event jumped out at me. The storyline was exactly the same until the moment when I decided to stash my bike in the bushes near Lincoln Point. In the original book I had ignored the prompting to hide my bike and had kept riding ahead. The gang along the road had tied me up and taken me to Mo. Therefore, I'd never met Tara. I was amazed at the changes that had come from heeding that one small prompting. I happily put the book down and sighed in relief, knowing I'd made the right decision. On one hand, I'd be back in the correct time if I hadn't followed the Spirit, but I sensed great events awaited me for doing so.

• • • •

Mom shook me awake. "Honey, there's something you need to see."

I groggily followed her to the temple lobby. The sun was shining, and all of the temple workers were gathered just outside the main doors. They were chatting nervously. I saw Dad standing near the fountain with Brother Newman. I noticed he was carrying his gun again.

As I walked toward them, a dull roar erupted from outside the temple grounds. I was shocked to see the entire temple block was surrounded by young people! They weren't happy, either.

"Your friends from Lincoln Point are here for a visit," Dad said with a sad smile. "Thankfully the electric fence is keeping them outside."

I was sick to my stomach. It looked like the whole horrible group from Lincoln Point had made the trip to the temple. "Have they made any threats?" I asked.

"Not really," Dad said. "They aren't too technically advanced. A few have tried to hit us with sling-shots, but we're too far away."

As we spoke, the crowd quieted down. At the bottom of the hill we could see someone being hoisted above the fence. Soon the No. 8 on his chest was in plain view.

"I want to talk to Eddie and the old man," Mo shouted.

"I guess you're the old man," I said.

Dad nodded. "Let's go closer and see what this Steve Young wannabe has to say."

We walked cautiously down the hill and Dad kept the gun ready. We got within 20 yards of the fence, and I could see Mo's eyes blazing. Dad raised the rifle to his shoulder and pointed it at Mo's chest.

"Hey, old man! What are you doing?"

"I'm just making sure your friends won't try any tricks," Dad called out. "If there's going to be bloodshed, you'll be the first to bleed." I gawked at Dad. The past few decades had really toughened him up.

Mo glanced around nervously. "Don't do nothing," he shouted to those around him. Then he turned again to us.

"Eddie, if you come back, my followers will leave this place alone," Mo said. "You and I can live together forever in Lincoln Point."

I couldn't help admiring his relentless confidence. He sincerely expected me to consider his offer. "I'm flattered you want me as your queen, but I'm not going anywhere."

This brought catcalls from the group. Mo stared angrily at me, then said, "If that's how you feel, we'll starve you to death. No one goes in or out of here! Your food train will get a big surprise the next time it comes. And if I get a chance, I'm going to kill all you old people. You outgrew your usefulness long ago."

Dad smiled and raised the rifle slightly. "Thanks for the warning," he called out.

Crack! Dad's shot skimmed Mo's shoulder pads, and Mo quickly jumped behind the fence. The crowd went nuts, and we hurried back inside the temple.

• • • •

Dad immediately called a meeting in the baptistry chapel. Twenty or so temple workers filled the benches. Everyone was there except four guards who were keeping watch on Mo's group.

I sat with Justin, Heather and Tara on the first row next to Mom. Dad stood before us, along with Brother Newman and another gentleman, Brother Miller. They were the temple presidency, and I could feel their united power.

Brother Miller opened our meeting with a word of prayer, then Dad stood before the group. "Brothers and sisters, we're facing a crisis, and I apologize," he said. "Times are hard enough, and now my family has brought this added burden upon you."

There were murmurs of "It's OK," and "We'll get through it," but all eyes were on Justin, whose head was bowed. He knew his selfish choices had created this mess.

Brother Miller raised his hand slightly. "I don't believe they could starve us out. We have almost a month's supply of food. They'll surely get hungry first and go elsewhere, since they only survive by raiding other cities. By the way, I've already radioed Jason and told him not to make any more deliveries here until further notice."

"Very good," Dad said. "I know they'll move on, but my fear is they'll start torching parts of Provo, such as BYU. I feel a duty to save those buildings, if possible."

I raised my hand. "I'm the one their leader wants. If I leave, the temple and BYU will be spared."

My comments caused a stir, but Dad shook his head. "I appreciate your offer, but that's not an option. Escape is impossible right now, and none of us would ever let you go back to Lincoln Point. There's no telling what you'd have to suffer through."

I glanced at Brother Newman, who seemed deep in thought. Then his eyes lit up. "Brother Dalton, what about the car?" he asked. "Maybe this is why it was brought here."

Dad's face also came to life. "I think you're right!"

I was confused. "There's a car here?"

"Yes," Dad said excitedly. "I'd forgotten about it, but two months ago a man drove a car to the temple gates. He introduced himself as a follower of Christ and said he had a delivery for me. He seemed honest, so we let him in. He pulled the car around to the temple's south side and backed it down the service entrance ramp. For a fleeting moment I feared I'd let in a car bomber, but when we caught up with the man, he was already covering the car with a plastic tarp."

"He just left it here?" I asked.

"Yep. He tossed me the keys and told me the tank was full, with four full gas cans in the trunk," Dad said. "The man said I'd know when to use the car. Then he somehow slipped away before I could talk with him."

"I got a strange feeling around him—a good feeling," Brother Miller said. "I'd never seen such piercing blue eyes."

"What was he wearing?" Tara asked. We all smiled at her. She'd hardly put two words together since she'd been tackled, so this was a positive sign she was recovering.

"I'm glad to hear your voice, Tara," Dad said. "Let's see, he was just wearing regular clothes—a flannel shirt and Levi's."

"I did notice he was wearing Nike athletic shoes," Brother Newman added. "I couldn't help wondering where he'd found such a nice pair."

The room was silent for a few moments as Dad looked right at me. "If you can get out of the gate you'd certainly be able to speed away from the mob," Dad said. "If they saw it was you behind the wheel, the mob would likely leave the temple and BYU alone."

Some of the brethren sounded skeptical. I think only Brother Newman and my parents knew who I really was. My parents had called me "Eddie" from the moment I'd returned from Lincoln Point, and if anyone had heard them call me anything else, they didn't seem to remember it.

"What are you saying, Brother Dalton?" one gentleman asked. "You're letting Eddie just take off? Does she even know how to drive?"

Dad chuckled. "Oh, she can drive." I knew he was remembering my high school days when I'd rammed our truck into a teacher's new car. "It'll be an adventure, but she can handle herself."

"That's fine," another man said, "but where would she go? Manti?"

"That's a possibility, but I think it's time she and the kids join the rest of our family."

Heather perked up. "We're going to New Jerusalem?"

"Exactly," Dad said.

Justin and Heather embraced, and the room was filled with excited chatter, but Tara looked glum. I put my hand on her knee. "I promised you we'd find your family. You're coming with us."

Tara tearfully embraced me. "Thank you. I didn't want to be left behind."

. . . .

By dawn everything was ready to go. The men had thoroughly checked the car—a blue Nissan four-door—and it was in pristine condition. Brother Newman turned the key, and the car chugged only a little before starting right up. The engine purred as if it were brand new. I checked inside and was glad to see it had an automatic transmission. I'd never mastered how to shift Doug's Volkswagen Bug without grinding the gears.

Several of the men commented they'd like to go for a test drive in the temple parking lot, but Dad wouldn't let them. "We need to keep this a surprise to that mob outside," he said. "Hopefully we'll catch them off guard."

The temple workers loaded part of the back seat with food and water, and we climbed inside. The girls took the back seat, while Justin took a seat beside me. I shuddered briefly, remembering that the last time I'd been in a car I'd been thrown through the side window. "Strap those belts across you," I told the kids. Dad gave me a knowing smile, and he helped the others figure out the seatbelt latches.

"Wow, I didn't know any of these machines still worked," Tara said. "Where did you learn to drive one?"

"My family once had a car," I said. "It wasn't this nice, though."

Dad smirked at my comment before saying, "Brother Miller was able to sneak down and unlock the gate. Then he slipped unnoticed into the little building near the gate. When he sees you approach, he'll turn off the electric fence and pull the gate open just enough for you to slip through."

"What if the mob tries to get in?" I asked.

"We'll be right behind you to push the gate shut again, and I'll have my gun just in case," Dad said. "Make sure they identify you, though, so they'll leave us alone."

"I guess this is it, then," I said nervously. Then an important thought struck me. "Which way do I go?"

"I've heard that I-80 from Salt Lake to Wyoming has been destroyed by the earthquakes, so you'll have to go south," Dad said.

"Just follow I-15 down to I-70, then work your way east the best you can. New Jerusalem is spreading in all directions, and the city should be halfway across Kansas by now, so just keep driving until you see friendly faces and new homes. Don't stop for any reason except for urgent bathroom breaks and to refuel. There are still a lot of bad people roaming the countryside."

"How long will the trip take?" I asked.

"Well, I doubt you'll be able to go too fast with all the road damage, but you might reach the outskirts of Zion by tomorrow if you drive all night."

"Thanks so much," I said. I hugged both Mom and Dad through the window.

"See you soon, honey," Mom said. I kissed her cheek then slowly drove the car up the ramp. When I eased into the parking lot only a few members of the mob were standing, but when they saw the car their excited shouts brought the whole mob to their feet. The majority of the hooligans hurried toward the gate. I rolled up my window and made sure all the doors were locked.

I reached the entrance as Brother Miller pulled the gate open. I expected an attack, but the mob just stared in awe at the car, unsure what to think. I looked in the rearview mirror, and saw the temple workers quickly get the gate latched behind me.

I proceeded at a snail's pace, trying not to run over anyone. I recognized the acne-faced kid whose helmet I'd ripped off, and I gave him a small wave. He just stared menacingly at me. Then I saw a surge of people coming from the north, with Mo at the head of the pack. I felt my anxiety level shoot sky-high, and I stepped on the gas, bumping a few people out of the way. Suddenly Mo's sneering face appeared at my side! He smashed his fist against the window, and I was amazed the glass didn't shatter.

That's all it took. I put the pedal to the metal and squealed the tires. The mob wisely parted, and the car rocketed down the street. We sped down the hill and turned south onto 900 East, leaving Mo and his wicked band in our dust.

Chapter Twenty-Five

My mind was racing after the close encounter with Mo, but I soon settled down and figured out my options. I didn't feel good about taking the Provo Center Street on-ramp, since we'd have to go back downtown. So I headed back over Ironton Hill and took the road leading to Springville's north freeway exit. There was so much rubbish and weeds clogging the road that I worried about popping a tire. I didn't dare go more than 25 miles per hour.

We nervously inched across the three deteriorating overpasses and then turned onto southbound I-15. It would've been easier just to get on northbound I-15, but I felt better being on the right-hand side of the road, even when the odds were zero that someone else would be driving down the freeway.

I soon realized the next overpass we'd see led to Lincoln Point. "Duck down below the window," I told the kids. "The Mighty One's guards are probably waiting ahead."

I pushed the car up to about 60 mph and got in the right lane, ready for anything that lay ahead. Men were standing on top of the overpass, pointing toward us. One picked up a big rock, fully intending to drop it on us. At the last second I yanked the car onto the off-ramp. We flew through the stop sign, bounced into the air and literally flew across 400 South. I somehow kept the car on the pavement as we rocketed onto the opposite on-ramp, and we were back onto I-15 before the warriors could even respond. In the rearview mirror I could see the warriors throwing tantrums over our escape.

I glanced back at the girls. They were terrified. "Please slow down," Heather tearfully pleaded. "You're scaring me."

"Sorry, but they were going to drop a boulder on the car," I said. "I'll go slower from now on."

"No, go faster!" Justin said in awe. "This machine is amazing!"

The next few hours were very uneventful. The hum of the engine put the girls to sleep, but Justin was captivated by every aspect of the car. He even pulled out the owner's manual and studied it thoroughly.

"Do you think I can drive this sometime?" he asked.

"Do you have a license?"

He crinkled up his brow. "Do you need one?"

"I'm afraid so," I said, knowing we'd never see a police officer. "Plus, you have to be 16."

He slammed a fist against his leg and muttered, "Shoot!"

• • • •

By 2:00 p.m. we had reached the exit onto I-70. I slowed down and watched for an ambush, but there wasn't anyone in sight. The area was returning to its original desert landscape. We soon were climbing into the mountains of central Utah. There were places where the road was broken up, obviously caused by a large earthquake. But previous travelers had created dirt roads around the debris, and we always managed to find a way through.

We crossed into Colorado during the late afternoon. The car was running well, but my right leg had started cramping up from holding down the gas pedal. I'd tried using the car's cruise-control, but the road was just too broken up for us to stay at one speed. The pain grew worse and I finally pulled to the side of the road.

"My leg is killing me, but it should feel better if I let it rest for a few minutes," I said. "Let's refill the gas tank and take our bathroom break." I limped out of the car and tried to shake out the cramp while Tara opened the trunk and removed the gas cans.

I hobbled up a small hill and stretched out on a patch of grass. Oh, it felt so good! I'd only been there for a few minutes when I heard the car's engine roar to life. I sat up to see Justin behind the wheel! Tara and Heather emerged from a nearby stand of trees just as the car lurched crazily backward.

"That little fool," I muttered. The car suddenly shot forward at an angle. Justin was trying to turn around! He nearly rolled the car into the barrow pit, but he braked just in time before putting the car in reverse again. However, instead of hitting the brakes this time he hit the gas, and the car rocketed off the pavement into a deep ravine.

Crash!

I joined Heather and Tara at the ravine's edge as Justin

shakily climbed out of the car, which was wedged squarely in the bottom of the ravine.

"Justin, what were you thinking?" Heather shouted. "I can't believe you did this!"

The boy was smart enough to keep his distance, and he climbed up the other side of the ravine. "I've decided I don't want to go to New Jerusalem," he shouted back. "I don't know how you convinced me to leave Lincoln Point, but I want to go back. That's where all my friends are."

"You consider those idiots your friends?" Tara yelled to him. "They beat you up!"

"You've lost your mind," Heather shouted.

I tried to keep calm as I called out, "Were you going to drive off without us?"

"I guess so," he said with a shrug. "I knew you wouldn't want to go back."

"You make me so mad," Heather shouted. "It's a good thing you're on the other side or I'd, I'd ..."

"Or what?" Justin taunted. "Kill me?"

"No, but I'd certainly tie you up," Heather shouted back.

Justin just laughed. "You wouldn't dare. Well, good luck with the car."

We stared in shock as Justin disappeared into a grove of trees. We scrambled down into the ravine, and while Tara and Heather checked on the car, I climbed up the other side. I still felt responsible for Justin, despite how horribly he'd been acting.

"Justin, please come back," I called out. "We can work things out!"

My shouts were only greeted by silence.

Chapter Twenty-Six

I watched for any sign of Justin for several minutes before finally accepting that he was gone. I slid down the slope to the car, and Tara threw her hands in the air. "We'll never be able to move this thing," she said. The rear bumper was resting on a boulder, leaving the back tires nearly two feet off the ground. We tried to push the car off the rock, but the car didn't budge an inch.

We finally collapsed in frustration. "This isn't fair," Heather said. "How could Heavenly Father let this happen?"

"Don't blame Heavenly Father," I said. "This was Justin's fault. In fact, maybe we should ask Heavenly Father for help." The girls gave slight nods, and we knelt the best we could next to the car.

"Heavenly Father, we humbly come before thee," I prayed. "We are in great need of thy assistance and protection. Please guide us in what we should do." I prayed for another minute before closing the prayer.

"What should we do?" Tara asked.

"I think we should stay with the car tonight, but in the morning we'll gather our supplies and start walking back to Provo. New Jerusalem is still too far away."

The girls climbed into the back seat, and I curled up in front. I was feeling pretty low. My errand wasn't going too well.

• • • •

"Hello down there!"

The shout snapped me out of a light sleep. I glanced in the back seat, where both girls were napping. I climbed out of the car and saw a man standing on the edge of the ravine. The sun was setting, and all I could see was his silhouette. He gave me a wave and started working his way down the slope.

"Heather, Tara, wake up! Someone's coming!"

I turned back to the man, who looked to be in his mid-20s. He was wearing a flannel shirt, Levi's, and Nike shoes. He had strikingly blue eyes, dark hair, and a clean-shaven face. He seemed strangely familiar.

The man put his hand on the car trunk. "It looks like you've got a problem," he said. "What happened?"

"My brother tried to steal the car, but he wrecked it," Heather said with a hint of embarrassment.

"Where's your brother now?"

"He took off into the mountains."

The man nodded, then walked around the car, inspecting the car's axles and frame. "I don't see much damage," he said. "I think we can move it, but I'll need your help. Let's push it off the rock."

"We already tried that," Heather said tiredly, but then she shrugged and joined the rest of us at the back of the car.

"When I lift the bumper, push as hard as you can," the man said. He pulled up on the bumper with both hands, and we pushed with all our might. The car inched forward a bit, then it slid off the boulder! The man brushed off his hands as the three of us danced around excitedly. "Thank you," I told the man. "You've saved us!"

"How are you going to get it back to the road?" he asked.

His question put a halt to our celebration as we peered at the steep walls of the ravine. I didn't know what to say, but the man said, "With your permission, I'd like to try driving the car out of here."

"Go ahead."

The man got in the driver's seat and motioned toward the top of the ravine. "Why don't you three go up to the road and stay clear," he said. "This could take some tricky driving."

We started climbing as he started the engine. We heard the car moving back and forth in the bottom of the ravine, but we were shocked when the man pulled the car onto the road even before we reached the top.

"How did he..." Tara stammered.

The man rolled down the window. "We're in luck! It wasn't as hard as I thought it'd be," he said. "Climb on in! I'll drive."

We numbly obeyed. Tara and Heather got in the back seat, and I sat next to this very peculiar stranger.

"Fasten your seatbelts," the man said, and suddenly we were traveling down I-70 again. The man stared straight ahead, and we were all still unsure what to say. Finally I said, "Thanks for helping us out. We could've never done it ourselves."

The man turned to me and smiled. "All in a day's work." His blue eyes shined. I recognized this man, but I couldn't place him. Within a few minutes we passed through the remains of Grand Junction, Colorado, and the man turned the car onto an exit marked "State Road 50." A few miles later he pulled onto a dirt road.

"Sir, where are you taking us?" Heather nervously asked from the back seat. "Do you know where we're going?"

"I sure do," he said. "New Jerusalem."

The man stopped the car next to the burned-out shell of an old barn, then he hopped out and disappeared inside. I pondered getting behind the wheel and leaving this helpful stranger behind, but within moments the man emerged pushing a large portable tank.

"Just refueling," he said casually. He filled the car's tank and then refilled the empty gas cans in the trunk. We stared in dismay at him, and he laughingly said, "This is my own personal stash." He soon put the portable tank back in the barn, and then we were again driving down State Road 50.

"Shouldn't you get back on I-70?" I asked.

"An earthquake collapsed the Eisenhower Tunnel last year," the man said. "Besides, you don't want to go through Denver. It's not a place for youngsters. It's worse than the lawlessness you faced there years ago, Emma...uh, I mean Eddie."

A warm feeling passed through me. This man knew my name! I stared at him and suddenly pictured him with a cloak and a beard.

"You helped us find shelter at Robber's Roost," I said in shock. "But how could that be? Do you 'travel' too?"

The man chuckled. "No, I don't travel like you do. I'm in this for the long haul."

The girls in the back seat were listening intently, and the man tilted his head toward them, signaling our conversation shouldn't be overheard. "Why don't you all just relax and catch some sleep," he said. "We've got a big day ahead of us."

It was now nearly dark, and the man flipped on the headlights. I suddenly felt the effects of the past two days weigh on me, and I drifted off to sleep, feeling strangely secure in the care of a man I barely knew.

Chapter Twenty-Seven

"Emma, wake up," the man whispered as he nudged my shoulder. "The others are asleep now."

I groaned and stretched, then snapped awake as I remembered this unusual man beside me. I glanced behind me, and the girls were snoring softly.

"I know you need your sleep, but I've been waiting so long to talk to you," the man said. "I'm Mathoni, remember? It's been a long time—more than 30 years."

I was confused. "What do you mean? I don't recall seeing you since 1868."

Mathoni got a worried look and moved his index finger in the air as if he was calculating something. Finally he said, "That's right! You're not there yet. Oh well, we'll see each other again by and by."

We cruised along for a few moments before I said, "I always get a warm feeling whenever you show up. Who are you? An angel? A resurrected being?"

The man shrugged. "I'm just Mathoni, a disciple of the Lord."

His name had a unique, ancient sound. Then it dawned on me. "Are you one of the Three Nephites?"

Mathoni cringed at that. "Well, my brethren and I are often called by that title. Mormon and Moroni never called us anything but 'disciples,' but we've somehow evolved into the Three Musketeers parading around destroying prisons and calming wild beasts. Actually, we rarely see each other."

"So what do you do?" I asked.

"I serve the Savior—that's my mission," Mathoni said. "For example, I've been assigned to help your family complete your errands. For the most part, you've done quite well and haven't needed my help. Of course, you had no way of knowing those guys at Robber's Roost would've taken your horses and tortured you to death, so I stepped in.

"And you've done a good job on this errand, but neither you

112

nor your father could have known that I-70 through the Rocky Mountains has been horribly rearranged. I had been waiting at Grand Junction to steer you onto this road for refueling until Justin decided to take matters into his own hands."

"Is Justin going to be all right?" I asked.

"I don't know," Mathoni said. "I'd love to assist him, but he's on his own until he humbles himself and asks for the Lord's help."

"That's what I figured," I said. "I feel like I failed him, but he has his agency. It was his choice to drive into that ravine and then leave us."

"Don't feel guilty, Emma. You've done very well. Some people are able to learn from the mistakes of others, but Justin isn't one of them. The poor boy will have to learn the hard way."

I tried to put Justin out of my mind by studying the landscape, which was completely flat. "Where are we now?" I asked.

"We're in Kansas. I got us past Denver and back onto I-70 during the night."

"Have you had a lot of these rescue missions?"

"Not really," Mathoni said. "I've spent most of my time over the years teaching people the basic gospel principles to prepare them for when the missionaries enter their lives. I just go wherever the Spirit leads me."

"Were you the guy who woke up my brother Doug in Manhattan?" I asked.

Mathoni chuckled. "Yes. That was one of my strangest 'short-term' assignments. Since Doug hadn't been born yet, I didn't even know who I was looking for. The Spirit directed me to a street in Jersey City, where I caught sight of a missionary sprinting out of a lady's house. He resembled your ancestor George, so I figured it must be Doug. He hid in some bushes, but when the police arrived he jumped over a wall and took off down a hill. That kid could run!"

I laughed. "So did you lose track of him?"

"I saw him climb into the back of a truck entering the Lincoln Tunnel," Mathoni said. "When I finally got across the river I couldn't find him among the crowds."

"Couldn't you just pinpoint him somehow?" I asked.

"I'm not magic," he said. "I prayed for guidance, and all I could sense was 'Central Park.' I searched the park all night and well into the next morning. I was about to give up when I saw some well-worn Sunday shoes sticking out from under a bush. It had to be Doug, since only missionaries wear shoes that've been destroyed that badly. Still, it was almost too late when I found him."

"It's a good thing you did," I said. "If he'd overslept and hadn't met up with Grandpa Keith's Army group..."

"Yes, it could've been a mess," Mathoni said. "Only later did I realize how close Doug came to missing that ship. Good thing he could run like a gazelle."

We paused as we heard Tara shift around and finally settle back to sleep. "I've got a question for you," I said. "How come you were wearing a cloak and sandals when I saw you in 1868?"

"Well, when I got the prompting to hurry to Robber's Roost I'd been teaching my Nephite descendants in Wyoming," Mathoni said. "I barely had time to build a fire in the cave before you started up the canyon. Besides, that cloak was comfortable."

I smiled and said, "It certainly helped keep the rain off you. But how come you were wearing a cloak again when you rescued Doug?"

Mathoni chuckled. "I admit I planned that. I was hoping you'd compare stories and wonder if it was the same person. Besides, I knew I'd be able to wear anything in Manhattan and get away with it—even in the 1940s."

I laughed as Mathoni's playful personality emerged. "You must get lonely," I said. "How do you cope with it?"

Mathoni frowned a little. "I'm not necessarily lonely, since I'm always mingling with people. I'd describe it more as a deep longing for my family. It was difficult when my wife and two daughters died, and then I outlived my grandchildren—and dozens of generations since. I don't have any complaints, though. I've been abundantly blessed by the Lord."

"Surely it hasn't been easy," I said sympathetically. "You seem mortal, but the scriptures say you were translated to a level somewhere between mortality and immortality so you could live until the Second Coming. That means you can't feel pain, right?"

"That's partly true," he said. "I don't feel physical pain, but I feel sorrow for the sins of the world. My first experience with that came when my civilization, the Nephites, turned against the gospel. I've never seen a civilization get wiped out so quickly. My people had lost the Lord's favor, and the Lamanites just slaughtered them.

"I spent a lot of time with the prophet Moroni, and we shed a lot of tears over the destruction of our people. Then when he died there wasn't a mortal left who held the priesthood and understood the fullness of the gospel. Once he was gone, the next few centuries really dragged by. When the Aztecs started doing human sacrifices, I just stayed clear of them and searched the world for anyone who still had a glimmer of light in their eyes."

"I would've taken off, too," I said. "Where did you go?"

"I first went to the Holy Land to see where the Savior had lived. Then I traveled to every part of the earth, which really isn't too hard to accomplish when you've got 2,000 years to do it," Mathoni said with a smile. "In fact, I spent a century in Europe helping to get the Enlightenment rolling, and since then the years have flown by. It seems like the Pilgrims landed at Plymouth Rock only yesterday."

He kept me entertained for the next hour with stories of his exploits, from being thrown into a blazing Lamanite furnace without being burned to playing a behind-the-scenes role in the formation of the United States. He also reminisced fondly about his periodic visits with Joseph Smith.

Mathoni said he spent the 1840s and 1850s helping the poorest Saints avoid starving to death, along with continuing to work among his descendants. In the past century he'd also played a big role in softening the hearts of civic leaders to allow chapels and temples to be built in their communities.

"Some of the Saints have written about visits with either you or your brethren," I said. "What seems strange is they often report seeing an older man with white hair. That obviously wasn't you."

Mathoni chuckled. "The other two translated Nephites were a bit older than me at the time of our 'change.' They think they look more dignified with a white-haired look, but I prefer my youthful appearance. Most of the stories you read took place in the 1800s when my brethren would dress in shabby clothes and stop by church members' homes to test their faith and charity by asking for a meal. If the members gave them food, they'd bless the home."

"Where were you at this time?" I asked.

"I was also around, but I was more inclined to plow a field at night for an injured brother or milk a cow for a widow," Mathoni said with shrug.

"You're an amazing man," I said. "I feel almost over-whelmed to know you."

"We're all part of the same glorious work, Emma," he said. "I don't think you comprehend the magnitude of this gospel. But you're about to get a taste of it."

Dawn had arrived, and Mathoni pointed ahead to some homes on the horizon. "We've reached the city's outskirts, my dear sister. Welcome to Zion!"

Chapter Twenty-Eight

I awakened the girls, and we all marveled at the pristine neighborhoods that covered the rolling hills. We drove on the highway for another 10 minutes before exiting into the city. An occasional bus was the only traffic we saw other than a light-rail train that passed above us on a bridge.

The streets were perfectly straight, running east to west and north to south, and they reminded me of Utah's streets. "The Savior always stays with the same community design," Mathoni said, seeming to read my mind. "It promotes order and unity."

I noticed a street sign that read, "23300 West" and pointed it out to Mathoni. "Is that sign right?" I asked. "Are we really that far from the city center?"

"Yes, we've got 233 blocks to go," he said.

The homes were made of light-colored brick that sparkled in the sun. They were mostly single-story homes with several variations, although there was an occasional two-story home. The houses' yards were narrow but very deep. Each lot was about 30 yards wide, with each house set about 25 feet back from the street.

This neighborhood was obviously a new addition to Zion, since the trees and shrubs were still small, but the front yards were filled with lovely flowers and a small lawn.

Mathoni slowed down for a moment and pointed behind a home where a man and woman were tending a garden. "Everyone has a large back yard where they grow fruits and vegetables. It allows most people to be nearly self-sufficient."

Something seemed missing, though, and I finally realized none of the homes had a garage or driveway. A simple walkway led from the sidewalk to the front door.

We drove alongside a bus, which was completely white except for the windows and two glass panels on its roof. I couldn't even hear its engine. Few buses are "glorious," but this one really was. I could see several people inside.

"Is that bus solar-powered?" I asked.

"Yes, as is nearly everything else in Zion," Mathoni said.

"You'll see some amazing technological advances while you're here. The Lord has poured out his spirit upon the people."

We soon approached two adjacent blocks that served as a community center. The blocks held a regular LDS chapel, a school and a library. There was also a light-rail station. Mathoni pulled into a small parking area and turned off the engine. "I hate taking this old gas guzzler into town," Mathoni said. "It just doesn't fit in."

We left the car and stepped inside the white-tiled station. It felt holy there, and we didn't speak as we absorbed our new surroundings.

Within three minutes a sleek light-rail train arrived at the station. Mathoni motioned for us to board, and we timidly climbed inside. Everything seemed to have a reverent aura, and I noticed Tara and Heather had their arms folded. I felt terribly under-dressed. I felt I needed to be wearing my Sunday best.

Mathoni greeted the train operator, a man with Asian features and bushy hair. "Please take us to the Temple Complex. My companions are newly arrived from Utah, and we're trying to find their families."

The driver smiled. "Welcome to Zion, my friends." The others on the train also greeted us kindly, and we took seats near the back of the train.

The train reached speeds of about 30 mph but ran silently. "Solar-powered too?" I asked Mathoni.

He nodded. "Amazing isn't it? I've seen more scientific progress in the last 100 years than I did in the first 1900 years combined."

We reached the crest of a hill and could see out beyond the city. Off in the distance to the north I could see bright red barns and some corrals every quarter-mile or so, with healthy fields of grain and corn placed around them.

"Are those barns part of Zion?" I asked Mathoni.

"Of course. New Jerusalem has been built just as the Prophet Joseph outlined in 1833," Mathoni said. "Joseph specified he didn't want any barns or stables among the homes of the people, which was wise. Joseph said he wanted the merchant and farmer to live side by side, so everyone could enjoy the benefits of society. It took the Saints almost 200 years, but we're finally completely following his guidelines."

After spending the last few days among Utah's ruins, this

city truly seemed like paradise. We stopped at a few more small "community squares" to pick up passengers or let them off. At each stop the driver would announce the location, such as "Pratt Plaza" or "Smith Square." Finally he said, "Next stop, the Center Place."

Within minutes we left the suburbs and moved among dozens of gleaming marble skyscrapers that filled the sky. The teenagers and I gawked at the splendor of the buildings. Mathoni enjoyed watching our expressions.

"I've never seen anything so beautiful," Tara said.

"Well, get used to it, because this is where we're getting off," Mathoni said. "Welcome to 'The Center Place of Zion.'"

The train entered a large granite terminal, and we cautiously disembarked. "I hope you find your family," the driver said kindly.

"Thank you," Heather said. "Have a nice day." We walked across a spacious indoor plaza. The ceiling was constructed to allow sunlight to filter in, and colorful flowers grew along the walkways. A large fountain sprayed skyward in the plaza's center.

"This is unbelievable," Tara said. "And everyone's so nice!"

We stepped outside and marveled at the beautiful buildings and landscaping. In the distance I could see a slender tower jutting into the sky, rising above any other structure. I pointed to it and asked, "Is that the temple? You know, Zion's main temple?"

Mathoni grinned. "It certainly is. Do you want to see it?" I eagerly nodded, and we set out for one of the most breathtaking sights I've ever experienced.

Chapter Twenty-Nine

We walked slowly down the gleaming sidewalk of a large boulevard. The bus traffic was heavier here, but it was hardly noticeable minus the noise and exhaust. We were eager to see the temple, but we kept getting distracted by our stunning surroundings. Every building was an architectural masterpiece, with every portion of extra space carefully landscaped with dazzling flowers. Even the city's citizens were interesting to observe. Many people wore white robes and were obviously refined.

"Some of these people are heavenly messengers," Mathoni said softly. "They're assisting the mortals with temple work by giving the names of those who've accepted the gospel in the spirit world. For the first two centuries after the church was restored, the Saints did temple work with the hope their ancestors would accept the gospel. But here in Zion, heaven and earth are so intertwined that we *know* who has accepted the gospel, eliminating the guesswork."

I watched some of these white-clothed people enter into a monstrous 25-story building with a sign above the entrance that said, "LDS Family History Center." The building didn't have windows, but was made out of a unique material that allowed us to see into the rooms. The first two floors were filled with rows of computers.

I kept my eye on one white-robed gentleman who entered the building and greeted a lady sitting at a computer. He handed her a sheet of paper and her face lit up, obviously delighted to receive the information.

We next saw a 200-member choir singing "Glory to God in the Highest" in a small alcove of the building. We paused to listen, and warm feelings flowed over me. I couldn't remember feeling happier.

"Come on," Mathoni finally said. "I'm eager for you to see the temple."

We rounded the corner of the Family History Center, and I was nearly knocked off my feet at the glorious sight. We stood before the New Jerusalem Temple, the most magnificent building I've ever seen. No other building on earth compares to it. I'll try to describe it for you, even though I won't do it justice.

The temple is actually a complex of 24 square buildings arranged in a circular pattern, covering dozens of acres. Each of these buildings alone was as large as the Provo Temple. From the inside edge of each of these buildings rose a sparkling 30-foot-wide metal arch that joined in the center with the other 23 arches to create an immense dome.

Immense glass panels filled the spaces between the arches, and at the pinnacle of the dome was the tall, slender spire I'd seen earlier. This spire easily reached 1,500 feet into the sky. Each of the 24 "compartments" was magnificent in itself, but the combined effect was mind-boggling.

We walked closer, and I was stunned to see there weren't any support beams on the inside of the dome—the arched design supported all the weight. The 24 buildings were connected at ground level by glass-enclosed walkways, but there were also elevated walkways that linked the terraced flower gardens that grew atop each of the buildings.

These gardens reminded me of the meadow and gardens that are atop The Conference Center in Salt Lake City. As magnificent as The Conference Center is, it's merely a practice run for the immense, awe-inspiring structures that will be built in Zion.

"I just can't believe anyone could build such a place," I said.

"It took some divine aid," Mathoni said. "Angels helped build this temple."

The whole complex seemed to shimmer in a cloud of glory. "The fame of this temple has spread worldwide," Mathoni said. "One unusual aspect of the temple is it appears to be immersed in flaming fire at night."

"How?" I asked. "That must take hundreds of lights."

"There are no lights," Mathoni said solemnly. "It is lit by the glory of God."

We spent an hour walking around the surrounding plazas. We approached the massive doors on the temple's east side, where the words "Holiness to the Lord" were engraved in the marble above the doors.

"Those doors won't be used until the Lord comes in His glory," Mathoni said.

"But isn't it true He visits here?" I asked.

"The Savior comes often to this temple," Mathoni said matter-of-factly. "This is His earthly house."

We saw a side entrance where people cheerfully filed inside. We desperately wanted to join them, but Mathoni gently informed us we needed temple recommends to enter. Unfortunately my recommend was somewhere back in Salt Lake, and I realized it had expired three decades earlier.

The glory of the temple had erased any other thoughts from our minds until Mathoni said, "It's time to find your families. I'm afraid I've got another assignment that begins quite soon."

Mathoni led us into a small building on the plaza that held a computer terminal. He punched a few keys, then said, "It looks like Tad and Emma North live within a few miles. Is that where you'd like to go?"

Heather smiled excitedly. "Yes, that's my uncle and aunt." Mathoni gave me a wink, and I had trouble catching my breath. We were going to *my* house.

• • • •

We boarded another light-rail train and headed into New Jerusalem's eastern suburbs. These neighborhoods were more established than the ones we'd passed through that morning. Mathoni was watching the street signs, and at 9400 East he pressed a buzzer.

"Hmm, I live on 94th East in New Jerusalem," I thought to myself. I'd never even thought that I'd have an actual home in Zion.

We exited the train and walked through a quiet, tree-lined neighborhood. Everything was lush, and a small stream ran between the road and the sidewalk. I'd seen several small ponds, and water seemed abundant, especially compared to the lack of water in Utah.

Within two blocks Mathoni pointed to a modest brick home. "There's the house," he said. "They'll be glad to see you."

We thanked him and each shook his hand. "You've been wonderful," I said. "Thanks for helping us get here and saving us all those other times. I'll never forget you."

Mathoni actually blushed a little. "It was my pleasure," he

said. "Well, I better get to that other errand. Enjoy yourself!"

Then he turned from us and walked down the street. The others hurried to the door, but I kept my eye on Mathoni. He glanced back at me once, gave a little wave, then vanished into thin air.

Chapter Thirty

A dark-haired man in his early 20s had opened the front door and was talking excitedly with the girls. Then he saw me walking up the path. He rushed past the others and gave me a hug. "Mom! I've sure missed you!"

I smiled at the man, not even sure which of my sons he was, but realizing I'd someday give birth to him. I took his hand and asked, "What did I name you?"

He laughed loudly. "I'm Charles, Mom. Wow, you look so young!"

The teenagers watched our exchange in disbelief. "How can she be your mother?" Tara asked him. "You look older than she does!"

Charles just shrugged and said, "Stranger things have happened." He led us into the front room, where a middle-aged man and a teenage girl greeted us. Beneath the wrinkles, bald head and slight paunch was my beloved Tad! He had aged, but he also looked very dignified

We immediately rushed to each other and embraced. "What has happened?" he whispered in my ear. "I expected a middle-aged Emma to show up here again."

"I guess I somehow altered the future," I whispered back. "Dad says this isn't how my book ends. I don't know what's going on, but I think I needed to bring the girls here."

Tad squeezed me tightly. "I'm just glad you made it safely."

The teenage girl timidly approached me. "Gee, I guess you really *were* my age once."

"You must be Leah," I said, remembering her name from when my parents had shown me my family picture at the Provo Temple. I pulled her close, hardly believing this radiant, golden-haired girl was my daughter. She kissed my cheek, and I covered my face with my hands as tears blossomed out of nowhere. Everyone became very concerned, but I smiled through my tears. "I'm just so very happy," I said. "I can't believe these wonderful people are my children."

"You deserve the credit for how they turned out," Tad said.

Meanwhile, Tara and Heather stood silently with shocked looks on their faces. I took Heather's hand. "Yes, I'm really your Aunt Emma."

She shook her head in disbelief. "The Aunt Emma I've seen in pictures is older and heavier. There's no way she could've wrestled that snake."

I laughed. "Well, have you heard of time travel?"

She said yes, so I continued. "When your father got home from his mission, we went to greet him at the airport. But we got in a car wreck before we made it there. I was thrown from the car—and into the future. We didn't have any children yet, and your parents hadn't even met."

Tara and Heather both seemed to quickly grasp the concept. "So you are Aunt Emma, just a younger version," Heather said.

"So where's your older version?" Charles asked.

"I'm not sure," I said. "I can only be in one place at a time, so I guess she temporarily doesn't exist. When I return to the right time, I'm sure she'll be back."

Tad put his arm around my waist. "Your disappearance here was a shock to me. Last Wednesday around noon you and I were rinsing some vegetables in the kitchen sink. I left the room for a moment, and when I came back the water was still running and the vegetables were on the counter, but you were nowhere to be found."

"It was about noon when I found myself thrust into the future," I said, piecing it all together. "So do the children know the whole story? Have they been expecting this?"

"They've read your book and we've explained it to them, but we've been waiting for the older Emma to return, not a 22-year-old version. This is really unexpected."

We heard a commotion at the front door, and suddenly three children burst into the room. "Charles must have called Dave. Come say hello to your grandkids," Tad said.

• • • •

My oldest son David and his wife Phyllis were naturally surprised at my youthful appearance, but I was happy to see them take our explanation in stride.

"It's a pleasure to meet you both," I said. "David, it looks like you've got a wonderful family. "

"Mom, just call me Dave," my oldest son said with a grin.

"All right," I said. "I'm a little behind on things."

He gave me a hug. "I'm glad you're safe. I'm sure the time-line will straighten out."

We spent several minutes catching up on things. David—excuse me, Dave—and his family lived on the next block. I also learned Charles wasn't dating anyone steadily, but that Leah did have a serious boyfriend, which surprised me. "Aren't you a little young, Leah?" I asked hesitantly.

"I'm 19 years old," she said a bit defiantly. "I thought you agreed it was OK."

Tad put his hand on Leah's shoulder. "Your mother hasn't yet experienced those discussions we had, honey." He leaned over and whispered in Leah's ear, and she smiled.

"Mom, let me ask you a question that should solve the matter for good," Leah said. I nodded warily as the rest of my family chuckled, seeming to know what she'd ask.

"OK, Mom," Leah said teasingly. "How old were you when you married Dad?"

I stammered a bit, and the room went silent. Finally I quietly said, "Nineteen."

The whole room cheered at my response, and Tad said, "She's got you, dear. Please remember this conversation and we'll never have to discuss this again."

The phone rang, and Tad hopped up to answer it.

"Mom, did you know that Dad is the bishop?" Dave asked.

"Really?" I responded in surprise. "I always knew he had the potential."

"It's a big job," Charles said. "He has to deal with every-thing in the ward, but he keeps it running smoothly."

"What about his other job?" I asked. "Is he still an accoun-tant?"

Charles seemed amused by my question. "We're living the Law of Consecration. Dad's calling *is* his job."

"What is your job, er...calling?" I asked.

"I help operate the farms outside the city's northeast quad-rant," Charles said.

I then asked Dave what he did. "I'm the Elders Quorum President," he said.

"That's it?" I asked. "That's your job?"

"Believe me, I wouldn't trade him," Charles said. "He's a busy guy."

I was a little perplexed. "So what do they pay you? Do you both make the same amount of money?"

They both furrowed their brows. "I don't understand your question," Dave said.

Tad cleared his throat in the hallway entrance. He'd finished his call and had been listening to our conversation. "They don't understand the term 'money' like you do," Tad said. "They also don't see one job being 'better' than another. We moved to the refuge in Hobble Creek Canyon when the children were young, and they've never known anything but the Law of Consecration."

"So it actually works?" I asked.

"Yes, and better than I would've imagined," Tad said. "The boys devote their days to their callings, and everyone in the church is assigned a role that fits their talents. For example, Leah is called to help a young widow care for her children, and I have my calling as bishop. We all serve the best we can, and we all receive whatever is sufficient for our needs. And when there's a surplus in the stake, it is shared equally."

I'd always heard of the Law of Consecration, but I'd never pictured it in operation. Tad could tell I was still a little confused. "Don't worry, it'll make perfect sense once you see it in action."

Charles stepped forward. "I hate to interrupt you, but Dave and I need to get to the ward softball game."

That's a sentence I never expected to hear in New Jerusalem. "I would've thought they'd outlaw church sports here," I said to Tad.

"The Saints still need recreation and exercise," he said with a smile. "The games here aren't the argument-filled, competitive battles we had to endure in Utah. Athletics and physical fitness still have their place in the Lord's kingdom, but winning is secondary to everyone having a good time. Besides, it's amazing how smoothly the games go here, since nearly all of the hot-headed trouble-makers stayed in Utah."

· · · ·

In all the excitement I'd forgotten about Tara. Heather found her napping in one of the bedrooms, and I knew it was time to reunite her with her family.

Before waking her, I explained the situation to Tad, wondering if we'd be able to locate her parents. "That shouldn't be too hard," Tad said. "All of the church members are listed on a central computer data base."

"Great! I'll wake her."

I went to the bedroom and knelt beside the bed. "Tara, are you ready to find your family?" I asked gently.

She sat up groggily, then nodded. "I didn't want to bother you as you talked with your family, but I'm anxious to find my parents. They probably think I'm dead."

"Come into the living room," I said. "Tad can help us locate them."

Tad was sitting at the computer terminal. "Hello again, Tara," he said kindly. "Let's type your parents' names into the computer and find out if they're here in Zion. What are their names?"

Tara moved to Tad's side. "I know my last name is Francom, but I've been struggling to remember my parents' first names. I just remember them as Mom and Dad."

"That's understandable," I said. "Just relax and hopefully the names will come back to you."

Tara closed her eyes and searched her memory, but nothing surfaced. Tad soon found all the Francoms in the city and pulled them up on the screen. There were about 15 families. Tara carefully scanned each name. Then she clapped her hands. "Mike and Samantha," she said excitedly. "That's them!"

Tad checked the address. "They live a few miles away, up on 130th East," he said. "Do you want to call them or just surprise them?"

Tara was so excited that she couldn't decide what to do. I finally said, "Let me just call and see if they're home."

Tad dialed the number and handed me the receiver. After four rings a woman answered the phone. "Hello, this is the Francoms. Samantha speaking."

"Hello, Sister Francom. My name is Emma North. I have a delivery to make to your home, but I'd like both you and your husband to be there."

"Mike is out in the garden. What's this about?"

"It's just a little surprise," I said. "I'll be there within 30 minutes, OK?"

"That would be fine," Samantha said. "See you then."

I hung up the phone and hugged Tara. "That was your mom. Let's go meet her!"

• • • •

Tara, Heather and I caught a bus on the corner, and 20 minutes later we were standing in front of the Francom home. Tara had chatted non-stop during the bus ride about memories of her family, but now she was very nervous and timid.

"What if they won't accept me?" Tara asked. "I've done so many bad things."

I saw the curtains move in the home's living room, and a woman briefly peered out at us. "If they turn you away, you can come live with us," I said. "But that won't happen."

Heather grabbed Tara's hand and led her to the doorway. Tara was shaking like a leaf as I knocked gently on the door, where a pleasant-looking woman greeted us.

"Are you Samantha?" I asked.

"Yes, and you must be Emma..." she said, but she couldn't get any more words out as Tara rushed forward and embraced her.

"I don't understand," Samantha said, looking at me.

"This is your daughter," I said softly, and Tara let out a sob. Samantha's eyes grew wide, and she grabbed Tara's shoulders and looked in her eyes.

"Tara? Is it really you?"

"Yes, Mom. I've missed you so much!"

They embraced again, and soon all four of us were sobbing happily. A man came to the door holding a glass of water. "What's all the commotion?" he asked.

"I'm home, Daddy," Tara said, and the man looked dumbstruck. The glass of water fell from his hand and splattered on the floor, but no one minded.

"Mike, our prayers have been answered," Samantha said.

Mike joined his wife and daughter in an emotional group hug. After a few moments, Tara backed away and said, "I've hoped you could forgive me. I was so awful to you before I ran away, and I've made some terrible mistakes since. I don't feel worthy to be called your daughter. Emma said I can live with her if you —"

Mike waved his hand. "Tara, don't talk that way. We love you and can barely express how happy we are to see you again. This is a dream come true!"

Heather and I stayed a few minutes longer, and we realized Tara was an only child. I couldn't begin to imagine the pain Mike and Samantha must've endured every day for the past several years. But I could see that torment ebb away as they chatted with Tara. The prodigal daughter had miraculously returned.

Chapter Thirty-One

We all agreed to stay in touch, and then Heather and I returned to the bus stop. I felt engulfed in joy to have witnessed that reunion. I also felt grateful for the privilege to actually be a part of the kingdom of God.

"Heather, go ahead and take the bus back," I said. "Just get off at 94th East."

"Are you sure?" she asked.

"Yes. I'm going to take a walk. Tell Tad I'll be there soon."

I waited until Heather got on the next bus, then I wandered into a small park and reclined on the grass in the shade of a tree. There was a small breeze, and the leaves rustled slightly. For some reason the rustling leaves sent my mind back to my 1868 visit in Charleston with Finity and Mary, the first Daltons to join the church.

My children were the eighth generation of that Dalton line to be members of the church, and I felt immense gratitude to each part of that family chain. So many things could've led any one of us off the narrow path, but somehow we'd stayed on. What if Finity's son George had decided to reject the church? Or if Keith had given in to the temptations he'd seen during World War II? Where would I be? Certainly not resting peacefully in New Jerusalem.

I thought of my own parents, who were teenagers in the early 1980s. Their biggest danger hadn't been warfare, but succumbing to peer pressure. What if they had actually believed "everyone was doing it" and had taken part in activities that would've destroyed their spirituality? Dad wouldn't have served a mission, and my parents likely never would've even crossed paths, since they first met at a church volleyball game.

I realized each generation had faced its own obstacles, and thankfully each one had conquered the challenges. Every family has similar stories, and each faithful generation adds another link to the chain that binds us all together. I hoped to someday thank my ancestors for staying true to the gospel, and I prayed I'd be worthy to join them.

. . . .

I finally caught another bus and returned to the house an hour later, where Tad was waiting for me.

"Heather told me you'd gone for a walk, but I was starting to get worried, " he said. "Did you get lost?"

"No, I just took some time to think," I said. "It's been quite a week."

"How did Tara's parents' react?" Tad asked.

"They were wonderful. Things will work out for them."

He nodded happily. "That's good. Well, I've got to go to the Bishop's Storehouse, and I was hoping you'd want to come along."

"Certainly!"

It was within walking distance, and we held hands as we traveled there. "I suppose a bishop in Zion is busier than earlier bishops were, correct?"

"Yes, but I think I've got it easier in some ways. Remember Bishop Nance when we first got married? He had his full-time job at the hospital, but then he still had his bishopric duties. So at least I don't have to worry about another occupation at the same time."

"I've read a little bit about the Law of Consecration," I said. "As bishop, aren't you in charge of allocating everything to everyone in the ward? Isn't that difficult?"

"When we first moved here, it was a very tough job, and I'm glad I wasn't a bishop then," Tad said. "People had a hard time shaking off their selfishness, and some people wouldn't consecrate everything to the church.

"For example, one woman had brought a beautiful set of china with her from Utah. The woman told the bishop she wouldn't give it to the church, since it had been her grandmother's china. The bishop told her she could keep what she needed, but that a family down the street had arrived without any plates or utensils. He asked her to share part of the china with the new family, but instead she took the whole set into the street and smashed it rather than share it."

"Wow, that was a little extreme," I said. "What happened to her?"

"She went back to Utah," Tad said. "I hope she's happy."

I pondered that story for a minute as we walked. "So let me

get this straight. Everyone consecrates what they have to the church, then they receive back what they need. Is that right?"

"Yes, people keep their own possessions, and we ask that they give their surplus to the Lord's kingdom. This surplus is evenly distributed, and the church members in Zion have reached the point where no one is in need. Most families have more than enough. Check out Leah's closet. She has plenty of clothes."

"Are there stores anymore?" I asked. "Or does everything go through you?"

Tad smiled. "No, I don't have to track every little item. Many people operate what could be called private enterprises, although the profits are consecrated back to the church."

"So I could get a new pair of shoes if I wanted?" I asked.

"Sure. We have bookstores, hair salons, bakeries, clothing stores, and so forth. Part of my calling involves assigning ward members an allotment that they can use as they wish. That way you can get the kind of shoes you want, and Leah can get the latest CD by 'Oz 3G' without upsetting the balance of having all things in common."

"What's 'Oz 3G?'" I asked.

"The most popular musical group in Zion," Tad said. "They're actually a third generation of singing Osmonds—the lead singer is one of Donny's grandsons. I've heard a couple of their songs and the music's pretty danceable. I especially like their remix of Grandpa Donny's song 'Puppy Love.'"

Tad then sang the new upbeat version of the song and did a little hip-hop dance along the sidewalk.

"Sounds pretty good. I'll have to check it out," I said with a laugh. "I'm glad to see you haven't become an old fuddy-duddy."

"Me? Never."

We walked past a rather large house, which sparked another question. "On a more serious note, how do you keep the housing equal? That would seem to be a tricky situation."

"I dealt with that issue just last week," Tad said. "One family in the ward, the Davidsons, arrived here 20 years ago with eight children under the age of 16. A large home was built for them. At the same time, a newly married couple, the Poulsens, built a small home on the same block.

"Now the roles are reversed. The youngest Davidson child just got married, and the Poulsens now have four children at home.

Things were getting a little cramped there, so I called Brother and Sister Davidson into my office and asked them if they'd be willing to switch houses with the Poulsens. They happily agreed, saying they'd felt similar promptings. And obviously the Poulsens were overjoyed about it."

"That's wonderful," I said. "No haggling over a price, and no hard feelings."

"You're getting the idea," Tad said with a smile.

• • • •

The moment Tad stepped into the storehouse there was no doubt he was in charge. He checked a few lists posted on a wall, then he called to a man stacking wheat sacks.

"Russell, did Brother Creer pick up his food allotment yet?" Tad asked.

Russell shook his head. "I'm afraid not. He called to say his wife had gone into labor unexpectedly, so he wouldn't make it here today."

Tad frowned, then guided me to another part of the building. "Are you ready to make a delivery?"

"What kind of delivery?" I asked.

"Well, first the food, and if our timing's right, maybe a baby, too."

We spent a few minutes loading a truck with groceries. I hopped in the truck as Tad gave Russell a few more instructions, then we drove to the Creer home. A woman on the porch told us the birth had been successful. We stepped inside and Brother Creer happily greeted us, then he gave me a startled look. "Sister North, are you all right?" he asked.

"She's lost some weight," Tad said hastily. "Now where would you like us to put the groceries?"

"Just on the table. Thank you for bringing the food," Brother Creer said humbly. "I didn't dare leave Cherylyn and the baby."

"It was no trouble at all," Tad said. "I see Cherylyn's visiting teachers have arrived, so you're in good hands."

Cherylyn wasn't ready to see visitors, so we soon left. I was ready to go anyway, because everyone kept speaking to me as if I should know their names and situations. I would nod and smile at them, realizing I'd suddenly become the bishop's wife, but I was horribly unprepared for the role.

We soon returned to the storehouse, and I helped sort cans of vegetables while Tad completed some paperwork. We returned to the house after dark and found Charles and Leah reading in the living room.

"Where's Heather?" I asked.

Charles pointed down the hall. "She was exhausted, so we moved a bed into Leah's room for her."

"Thanks, son," Tad said. He then headed to the bedroom, but I was curious to see what the kids were reading. They were each reading a thick book with a gold cover.

"Are those the scriptures?" I asked. Charles handed his book to me. "Well, yes," he said. "But I suppose you've never seen this volume."

I held the cover to the light. It read: *The Record of the Ten Tribes.*

"Whoa, I can't believe it!" I exclaimed. "Where did you get this?"

"At the bookstore," Leah said. "Everyone has a copy, Mom."

"That's amazing," I said. "When did the Ten Tribes get here?"

"They arrived in Zion about three years ago," Charles said. "It doubled the city's population overnight, and the temples were overflowing for months as they did temple work for themselves and their ancestors."

"Where were they living for all those centuries?" I asked excitedly.

Leah looked a bit exasperated. "Just read the book, Mom."

Tad's voice called from the bedroom. "Come to bed, dear. It's been a long day."

I wanted to read that book, but the kids had settled back onto the couch. So I gave Charles back his book and went to the bedroom, where Tad was already in bed, reading the newest *Ensign* magazine.

"Why isn't everyone excited about the return of the Lost Ten Tribes?" I asked as I sat on the edge of the bed. "This is the first time anyone has even mentioned it all day!"

Tad smiled a little. "Believe me, it was pandemonium around here when they first arrived. But I guess it's similar to when we were younger. Everyone always talked about what a major event it would be when Russia allowed missionaries to preach there. And what happened?"

"After the Berlin Wall fell, Russia was soon opened to the missionaries."

That's right," Tad said. "It was a significant event, but it soon just became part of history. The same thing has happened here with the Ten Tribes."

"I see your point," I said. "But where have they been?"

"I'll just say they weren't on another planet or living under the polar ice cap, as many people had theorized. They'd been living as a group, but hidden from the eyes of the world. So when they began their journey here it really caught everyone's attention, since they seemingly emerged out of nowhere. As they came from the north, ice literally flowed away and a natural road was cast up. We had a few days' notice that they were coming, and we gave them an incredible welcome. It was an unforgettable day."

"So where are they now?"

"They've built homes here and have become part of this glorious society."

I pondered for a moment. "The driver of the train we rode on this morning had a unique look about him. Could he have been one of them?"

"Probably so," Tad said. "They built most of their houses on the western side of the city."

"Thanks for answering my annoying questions, dear. You've been very patient with me."

Tad laughed in surprise. "I don't mind. It's actually been fun."

Tad and I then knelt together to say our prayers, but as we climbed into bed everything started to feel very weird. I couldn't bring myself to kiss him good-night.

"What is it, honey?" Tad asked.

"Don't you feel a little strange?" I asked.

He started laughing and rubbed his eyes. "I thought it was just me. I know you're my wife, but you're not quite the spouse I'm accustomed to."

"I feel the same way," I said with relief. "I'm surprised the children didn't seem bothered that we'll be sharing a bed."

"Why would they?" Tad said. "You're their mother. You've

been gone for a few days—and you somehow lost a bunch of wrinkles and a lot of weight—but otherwise everything is back to normal."

"I still feel uncomfortable..." I said.

"Oh, so do I," Tad quickly agreed. "I feel as if I'm cheating on you. The Emma who usually lives here is the greatest woman I've ever known, but let's just say I haven't had a figure like yours in my bed for more than 20 years. I think I'm coveting my own wife."

"Tad! I can't believe you'd say that!" I said in shock. "Control your thoughts!"

I tried to push him out of the bed with my feet, but he wouldn't budge. "Let me finish," he said hastily. "Along those lines, you've been very kind not to comment on my appearance. I realize I no longer resemble the Tad North that made you click your heels together. I feel like I'm your grandpa."

I shook my head in surprise. "I guess women aren't so hung up on looks, because ever since I saw you today I've been amazed at how dignified you are. You're a man that everyone loves and respects." I put my arm across his shoulders. "You've developed into such a wonderful person. The 24-year-old husband I left in Salt Lake might have well-toned muscles and all of his hair, but he's only begun to develop his true potential."

"So you're not disappointed in how I've turned out?" Tad asked meekly.

"Not at all! Actually, you've turned out better than I expected."

"Thanks a lot!"

"I'm sorry. That came out wrong," I said with a laugh. "Let your mind go back to our first year of marriage. Who did our grocery shopping when I broke out in hives?"

He pondered a moment. "I think your mom did."

"That's right, because you couldn't put a shopping list together. Now you run a Bishop's Storehouse like you've done it your whole life! Do you see what I mean?"

Tad smiled. "I understand."

"I'd also like to make a promise to you," I said. "I'll watch my weight a little more closely. What caused it, the pregnancies?"

He shrugged. "A little, but not really."

"What happened then? Tell me!"

He cautiously said, "Don't worry about it. You're a wonderful cook, and I'd hate for you to cut back on the delicious meals you make."

I eyed him carefully. "You're holding something back. What is it?"

He gave in and said, "Maybe make only a single batch of cookies at a time, instead of a big double batch that we end up eating all at once."

I winced. I'd developed a sweet tooth after we got married, although it hadn't affected my figure during the first couple of years. "I'll keep that in mind," I said ruefully.

We laughed for a moment, then Tad asked, "How are we going to handle this marriage arrangement? You could be here for a while."

"I feel we should act like best friends, but nothing more," I said.

"Aw, really?" Tad said. "Not even a good-night kiss?"

I leaned over and gave him a little peck. "That's all, though," I said. "I'm serious about this! you'd better stay on your side of the bed, or I'm sleeping on the couch."

Chapter Thirty-Two

The next morning I opened my closet, but all my clothes were much too big for me. I pulled on an oversized robe and walked down the hall to Leah's room.

The door was open slightly, and I could hear the girls talking. "Knock, knock," I said. "May I come in?"

"Of course, Mom," Leah said. "What's up?"

"Well, I was wondering if..."

"You need some clothes, don't you?" Leah said with a smile. "Let's see what we can do."

Heather also needed a new wardrobe, and the three of us spent the next 30 minutes mixing and matching items. Leah's clothes were quite stylish, with bright colors and interesting patterns. I'd often wondered if the Law of Consecration would limit the Saints to drab, gray clothing, but this wasn't the case.

Leah had several modest skirts, which seemed to be the fashion for teenage girls in Zion. She only had a few pairs of pants, and there wasn't a mini-skirt in sight. Leah's shirts were also very modest, with no dipping necklines or sleeveless tops. It was a relief to see my daughter's wardrobe as I remembered some of the immodest fashions of my generation. I was glad the pendulum had swung back the other way—at least in Zion.

I finally selected a navy blue skirt and a bright red shirt for myself. "Are you sure that's what you want to wear?" Leah asked me.

"I think they look good together. Don't you?"

"Certainly," Leah laughingly said, "but just last month you told me that combination was 'too flashy.'"

"Well, I've changed my mind."

I put on some sandals before saying good-bye to the girls, who were still trying on clothes. I found Tad in the kitchen making breakfast for us. "Nice outfit," he said as he buttered some toast.

"Thanks," I said. "Leah was very gracious with her clothing."

We sat at the table and enjoyed a meal of oatmeal, toast, and sliced apples. Charles passed through while we were eating and gave us each a kiss on the cheek. "I'm off to the farm," he said happily. "See you tonight."

"Have a good day, son," Tad said.

Once he was gone, I returned to a subject that still confused me. "Was Charles forced to be a farmer? Couldn't he do something else?"

Tad sat up straight and gave me a worried look before visibly relaxing. "Whew! For a moment I forgot that you're the 'young Emma,' with a pre-Zion mentality," he said. "The Emma I usually live with is very happy with what Charles does."

I frowned. "I guess 'the corporate ladder' and 'money equals success' got subtly ingrained into me over the years, didn't it? I mean, we sacrificed a lot to put you through BYU so you could earn a good living. I see those ideas don't exist in Zion, though."

"We're finally living the Law of Consecration the way it was designed," Tad said. "Don't think it was easy at first, though—even for the most faithful Saints. We all had the mentality you just described, since that's how we were raised. Many people couldn't adjust, and they left the church. But the rest of us worked out our problems, and the children who have grown up in this society are splendid, charitable, loving people. Charles and Leah are much more spiritually attuned than we ever were at their ages."

"I still don't see the whole picture," I said. "Are people assigned their jobs? What if you don't like your job?"

"First of all, every child in Zion receives an outstanding education. The school curriculum is inspired. Much of what you and I learned in school was tainted or inaccurate, but the children in Zion's schools get straight truth, and unnecessary classes have been eliminated."

"I hope they got rid of Trigonometry," I said.

Tad laughed. "It's still taught, but in a much more enjoyable way. It is used to explain the structure of the universe and such things."

"So Trigonometry does have a purpose!"

"Yes, believe it or not," Tad said. "I've often wished I could've gone to school here. By the time our children finished high school, they were more knowledgeable and well-rounded than I was after graduating from BYU. If you really want to be impressed, just ask Leah to explain the organization of the galaxy for you."

"She'd probably blow my mind, " I said with a grin. "So does anyone go to college?"

"We have a few colleges where people receive specialized technical training, but for the most part when a person finishes high school they move into society and begin to contribute. We don't have any 'professional students' in Zion."

I nodded thoughtfully. "So that brings us back to Charles. How did he end up as a farmer?"

"This is really bothering you, isn't it?" Tad said with a laugh. "Give yourself 30 years and you'll accept it wholeheartedly. But in Charles' case, he loved being outdoors almost from birth. By the time he was 12 he had his own garden plot in our back yard. We encouraged him in that direction, and now he's one of the best young horticulturists in Zion. He gets 10 times the production out of this soil than did the people who tilled it 100 years ago."

"You've convinced me," I said with a smile. "Life seems so wonderful here. People seem so happy and relaxed."

"The great thing about the Law of Consecration is that equality brings happiness and more time for your family," Tad said. "I think back to the 1990s and just shake my head. We were all running around like chickens with our heads cut off, trying to outdo each other and make the most money. The rest of the world continued on that path, and you can see how that ended up."

We were briefly interrupted as the girls entered the kitchen. "I'm going to introduce Heather to some of the girls in the ward," Leah said with a radiant smile. "We'll be back in a while." They each grabbed an apple and quickly departed.

"Leah is amazing," I said. "She actually glows."

Tad looked up from his cereal. "Her mother deserves most of the credit."

"It's hard to believe I raised that girl," I said. "I don't know a thing about parenting."

"Just keep that beautiful young woman in mind when as a baby she throws her bowl of food across the room, or scribbles all over the wall," Tad said. "All of your kind parenting shows in Leah's face. Would you like some more toast, dear?"

I nodded, and he went to the kitchen. I was feeling a little overwhelmed to see how my family had turned out. I was happy, of course, but I also felt undeserving.

When Tad returned I asked, "Fill me in on a few things. Life obviously hasn't always been this cozy. My parents said we were one of the first families called to build Zion. What was left in this area when we arrived?"

Tad shrugged. "Not much. The people who'd lived here had been either killed or driven away by floods, tornadoes, or civil unrest. When we arrived here in our wagons there wasn't a single living soul."

"We came by wagon?" I asked.

"Well, there wasn't any gasoline. Plus, the roads were destroyed, and the railroads were mangled by the earthquakes. Of course, our wagons rode a little more smoothly than our ancestors' wagons did. Our wagon had cushioned seats, shock-absorbers and steel-belted radials—after we dismantled our van in your parents' front yard."

I laughed in surprise. "That explains the car parts I saw near Doug's Volkswagen. I thought vandals had done that!"

"Nope, we did it ourselves," Tad said with a smile. "Even though the citizens were gone when we got here, most of the buildings were still intact, especially on the Kansas side of the river. Our electrical engineers got Kansas City's power grid working within a week, and your dad's skills as an electrician came in handy. He did a lot of repair work."

I tried to picture that exciting time. "So what did we do? Your accounting skills probably weren't of much use without taxes to worry about."

Tad chuckled. "I still used my counting skills everyday—I counted each of the 400,000 bricks I laid in a two-year period."

"You were a bricklayer?"

"Yes, and I must say I was one of the best," he said proudly. "You and the children stayed in a Kansas City apartment building while I joined other fellow 'unemployables'—you know, the car salesmen, the office workers, the real estate agents and the like. We toned up our flabby muscles and literally laid the foundation for this spectacular city. I'd visit you each Sunday, but otherwise I worked 10 hours a day to get Zion underway."

"And now look at how it has grown," I said, peering out the window at the majestic downtown area to the west. "Did you get to work on the temple?"

"Thankfully yes," he said reverently. "It was one of the

greatest experiences of my life. I finally realized how the Saints felt who built the Kirtland and Nauvoo temples. We were on a special errand, and our Savior was well aware of our efforts. Miracles happened almost daily."

"This seems like a fairly new neighborhood," I said, looking out at a house across the street. "If we were among the first ones here, how come we live so far away from the temple?"

Tad swallowed a bite of toast, then said, "Our first home in Zion was actually where the Center Place train terminal now stands. But as more and more people began pouring into Zion, you and I—along with many of our Springville friends—were called to settle an area several miles east. There wasn't much here when we arrived, but we built homes once again, and within five years the area between us and the temple complex was filled with homes."

"Where did all the people come from?" I asked. "Certainly not just Utah."

Tad smiled as his thoughts returned to the exciting times of New Jerusalem's early days. "Zion got a huge boost when the Saints from Central America and South America finally arrived here. Most of them had to travel on foot, so it took them a while longer to get here following the prophet's general call to Zion. But they brought an energizing, pure spirit with them, and that's when New Jerusalem began to feel like a Zion community."

Tad tried to blink away a tear, but it slipped down his cheek. "We're so blessed, Emma. Once you return to the past, keep us on the right path. If I slack off or murmur, give me a swift kick in the behind. Don't let us miss this glorious experience."

Chapter Thirty-Three

Later that week I attended church with the family. Tad had explained that the standard three-hour meeting block was still in effect. "And yet that old rumor still persists that we'll drop Sunday School and just have two hours of church," he said with a laugh. "Some members are still clinging to that hope."

The ward met in a beautiful chapel built on the top of a knoll that overlooked the city. As we approached the entrance, a young family struggled to herd their five children through the building's doors. I quickly realized that a child in Zion will still have the same lovable noisy traits as today's children.

We entered the chapel for Sacrament Meeting, and many of the ward members greeted me kindly. They seemed a little surprised that I didn't know their names, since I was obviously Sister North, the bishop's wife—minus several pounds and wrinkles. Finally Charles pulled me onto a pew to save me from further embarrassment.

Leah soon arrived on the arm of a handsome young man with blond hair and brown eyes. "Mom, I'd like you to meet Greg," she said.

He nervously shook my hand. "Hello, Sister North. We've met before, but Leah says you don't remember me."

"That's true, but I can see why Leah likes you so much."

Leah smiled at my approval, and they quickly settled next to me on the bench. Once the meeting started, Tad took care of the ward business from the pulpit. He announced the opening hymn then said, "I forgot to mention one item of business. Most of you have noticed that my wife Emma doesn't seem to be her usual self today. There's a reason she doesn't know any of your names. The Emma you see here today is the young woman I married long ago, rather than the Sister North you're all acquainted with."

There were murmurs throughout the congregation and a man called out, "What do you mean, bishop?"

Tad then eloquently described my situation, and these

wonderful people began to nod approvingly. When you've seen angels help build your temple and had the Lost Ten Tribes roll into town, a time-travel story isn't too hard to accept.

"We don't know how long this situation will last," Tad said in conclusion. "It could end tomorrow, or it could go on for a few weeks. Either way, I know you'll introduce yourselves and make Emma feel welcome. I'm grateful to be your bishop, and thank you for all the good work all of you do."

Tad sat down, and the entire congregation turned in my direction, smiling and waving. I blushed and waved back, surprised at their heartfelt response.

The whole meeting was uplifting, but the highlight for me was when my son Dave's five-year-old daughter Kiffon left her parents—who were seated in the pew behind us—and climbed onto my lap. She carried an illustrated children's book. I read the back cover, and the book apparently followed a boy's journey from Utah to New Jerusalem. "This book's about my daddy," Kiffon whispered.

"Oh really?" I asked.

I turned the book over and read the front cover, which showed a young man pulling a handcart up a rocky canyon. The title read:

Dave's Decision
by Emma D. North

"In the book, Daddy chooses to follow the Lord," Kiffon whispered. The book's cover blurred before my tear-filled eyes, and I tenderly kissed my granddaughter's precious cheek.

"I'm glad your daddy made that decision," I said, hardly able to control my emotions. I felt Dave put his hand on my back, then he gently squeezed my shoulder as he whispered, "You still write better than ever, Mom."

• • • •

I did my best to get to Sunday School, but I spent the entire time in the foyer as family after family greeted me and introduced themselves. A few of the older couples were people I'd known growing up in Springville. As Tad had previously explained, most of the ward consisted of former Springville residents or their descendants. It was interesting to see the same names crop up: the Johnsons, Crandalls, Birds and Miners seemed as prevalent in this ward as they had been in Springville. But there were also people in the ward from places such as North Dakota and Alabama. It was interesting to hear their stories of perseverance during the nation's collapse, and then to see the joy in their eyes as they described arriving in Zion. The Lord's hand was evident in every story.

• • • •

Leah came to my side as Relief Society was about to begin. "I introduced Heather to the Young Women leaders," she said. "She's making friends with many wonderful girls—and the boys are taking notice of her, too."

"I'm sure of that," I said.

We entered the Relief Society room just as the lesson was starting, and Leah pulled her lesson manual out of her bag. I was pleasantly surprised to see a familiar face on the cover, which read:

Teachings of Presidents of the Church
Gordon B. Hinckley

"Oh, how wonderful," I said. I took the manual from Leah and opened to the introduction. It summarized President Hinckley's life, and concluded with these paragraphs, as far as I can recall:

"President Hinckley was instrumental in bringing the church from relative obscurity to worldwide recognition. His pleasant personality and openness with the national and world media created opportunities for the church to be recognized in a positive way across the globe.

"His inspired concept of building smaller temples came as the church's FamilySearch program was being made available to the world on the Internet. The two projects combined to help accelerate family history and temple work to unprecedented levels.

"Among his accomplishments as prophet included the First Presidency's Proclamation on the Family, which helped strengthen and prepare the Saints to survive the difficulties of the

early 21st Century.

"He will also always be remembered for envisioning and overseeing the construction of the magnificent Conference Center east of Salt Lake City's Temple Square. The building was completed in the year 2000 and set a new architectural standard among church buildings. It was the prototype for the awe-inspiring edifices that the church has since built in New Jerusalem.

"An interesting sidenote is that the Conference Center's pulpit was built from a black walnut tree President Hinckley himself had planted in his yard 36 years earlier. The tree had recently died as The Conference Center neared completion, and the idea was put forth to use the tree's wood to build the pulpit. Approval was given, and the finished product served as a beautiful reminder of a marvelous prophet.

"Although the Conference Center is temporarily closed until the Millennium, that same pulpit is still operational, and President Hinckley's personal contribution to the building will likely last for countless more generations."

I handed the manual back to Leah. "That only begins to mention his accomplishments," I whispered. "What an amazing man."

That night we gathered at our home to celebrate the birthday of Dave's wife Phyllis. She was an attractive woman with sandy-blonde hair who'd passed her pretty features on to the grandchildren.

Heather and Leah had baked a birthday cake, and we had a fun evening together. Then I innocently opened up old wounds.

"Phyllis, where are your parents?" I asked. My question brought the whole room to a standstill. Tad came to my side. "This is a happy occasion, dear," he said gently. "We'll discuss this another time."

Phyllis held up her hand. "No, it's OK," she said. "I'm sure Heather doesn't know the story either, so I'd prefer they heard it from me."

Dave came to his wife's side to offer support as Phyllis began her story. "I was raised in Baltimore, Maryland. My family wasn't LDS, and money and prestige were all that mattered to my parents. We lived in an upper-class neighborhood, and my life seemed great. I was 20, attending college and driving my own sports car. But World War III changed everything. We stayed tucked away in our home for months, and when the war ended we realized Baltimore wasn't a very good place to be."

Phyllis paused for a moment as Dave handed her a tissue. "My family watched the scary news reports about the post-war riots and decided to remain in our home as long as possible. We had enough food to live for a few more weeks, but within days the looting mobs moved into our neighborhood.

"One morning six men broke down our door. My dad and brother tried to stop them, but both were stabbed to death as I watched from the top of the stairway. I ran to my bedroom window, climbed out onto the roof, and literally hid in the top of the chimney. It was safe there, but it was also horrible, because I could hear the dying screams of my mom and sister echoing from below. Soon all was quiet, but I stayed in the chimney until dark."

She paused again to collect herself, and I tearfully looked around the room. Everyone else was crying, too.

"Phyllis, I'm sorry I asked," I said. "You can stop now."

She shook her head. "It's good to talk about it once in a while," she said with a sad smile. "It reminds me of the Lord's hand in my life. Anyway, after dark I left the neighborhood and just kept moving from bush to bush, trying to stay hidden. When sunrise came, I realized I was downtown. The air was thick with the smell of death, and I was horrified at what lay before me. There were piles of dead bodies all throughout the downtown parks. I hid myself under an abandoned car and watched in terror as people killed each other for no reason at all. Mothers killing their children...it's too horrible to describe more."

"Then how did you get here?" Heather asked tenderly.

"I stayed under that car all day, but that night I headed south," Phyllis said. "For some reason I felt I needed to get to Washington D.C., although I had no hope it would be better there. Within a week I reached the 495 Beltway—the old freeway that circled the city. I hadn't seen anyone for a day or so, and I realized the nation's capital had been abandoned. In despair I just started walking along the freeway, hoping to see any sign of life. I was almost convinced I was the last person on earth. Then I saw the spires."

"The Washington D.C. Temple?" I asked excitedly.

Phyllis smiled. "That's right. I had a strong feeling that I had to reach that building. When I arrived, there were about 500 people camped on the temple grounds. It was such a relief to see humans who weren't stabbing each other. I timidly approached the group and a man walked toward me. He said, 'Welcome, dear sister. Would you like to join us?' I collapsed with relief to meet someone who didn't intend to kill me, and Brother Fox carried me to his family's tent."

Tad put his hand on my shoulder. "Remember Doug's pal Billy Fox? He's the one who welcomed Phyllis into his tent."

"Billy Fox?" I asked in shock. "What was he doing out there?"

"Billy had been going to medical school at George Washington University when the war broke out," Tad said. "Once it was over, he helped people gather at the temple, and he organized a group to journey to Utah."

"In fact, his group left the day after I arrived, and I went with them," Phyllis said. "By the time we reached Illinois, more than half the group had died from various illnesses and fatigue. Brother Fox felt our group was getting too small to still intimidate the gangs roaming the area, so we headed to Nauvoo, which was also abandoned except for the guards who were protecting the rebuilt Nauvoo Temple. These guards informed us a group of Saints from Utah was moving east to build New Jerusalem! I didn't understand what that meant, but the rest of the group was very excited. We rested and regrouped for a few days, then we set out for Missouri."

Dave raised his hand. "I'll finish the story, if you don't mind," he said with a grin. "Billy's group joined our camp about two weeks after we arrived here. We were glad to see the new faces, and one face in particular just blew me away." He smiled at his wife. "I couldn't get Phyllis out of my head."

"I thought Dave was cute, but he seemed so young!" Phyllis added. "I was now in my early 20s, and he looked about 16!"

"It was my boyish good looks," Dave said. " I was actually nearly 18 at the time."

"So you married an older woman?" Heather asked with a surprised laugh.

"Yes, with no regrets," Dave said. "I actually helped teach her the gospel, which was really just an excuse to be near her. I only wish she'd accepted my marriage proposal as quickly as she had accepted being baptized!"

Chapter Thirty-Four

I pondered Phyllis' story that night as I lay in bed. She'd been through some of the worst events of modern times. The world had changed so much in such a short time. The only functioning form of government left on earth was found in the church. Tad had explained how the Saints still upheld the Constitutional principles as set forth by the Founding Fathers. As the United States government crumbled, the church had out of necessity taken the roles of both church and state.

I nudged Tad with my elbow. He awoke with a start. "What is it?"

"Tell me about holidays now," I said. "Do you still celebrate them?"

Tad looked a little perturbed to be awakened by such a question, but he propped himself up in bed and said, "Why do you ask?"

"Well, Phyllis mentioned how Washington D.C. was abandoned, so we probably don't have all those federal holidays now. What about Labor Day?"

Tad shook his head. "No, somehow that one hasn't survived."

"Surely we still celebrate Christmas," I said.

"Well, yes, but it's toned down considerably," Tad said. "Before the war, Christmas had become so commercialized that you hardly heard the Savior mentioned. So now we're back to the basics, with just a few decorations, along with the traditional manger scene. And Easter is solely devoted to remembering the Savior's resurrection."

"That makes sense," I said. "So I'm guessing Santa Claus and the Easter Bunny have made their final rounds?"

"I'm afraid so."

"Hmmm. What else has changed?" I asked.

"Actually, April 6th is one of our bigger holidays now. It's known as Restoration Day, because that's the date the church was restored in 1830. We have parades, picnics and special programs. April 6th is also generally accepted as the Savior's actual date of birth, which makes the day so much more significant."

"What about Halloween?" I asked. "Did it get the ax?"

"Yes, mainly because we were so busy harvesting the crops and building homes those first couple of years that it just got forgotten. Besides, the holiday's darker elements just didn't seem to belong in Zion."

"I understand," I said. "It would be really weird to see vampires and witches wandering these streets."

"We still know how to have fun, though," Tad said. "Our New Year celebrations are really festive. We get together as wards for games and food, then at midnight the city puts on a fireworks show that beats anything you've ever seen."

• • • •

I spent the next few weeks settling into home life—in my own home. I had been surprised to find that the little wooden horse John had carved for me in Denver during 1868 was still on my bedroom dresser. That small sculpture was now an antique.

I chuckled at myself as I saw some of the habits I'd retained over the years. I checked the linen closets to discover I still folded the towels the same way, and I still used the kitchen's top left drawer as a junk drawer. I noticed a few of my other quirks—and Tad's—had also continued through the years.

When we first got married, Tad agreed to always load the dishwasher if I'd unload it. I appreciated his help, but his haphazard style of loading the dishes had always irritated me a little. We'd discuss it, but his style never changed.

One afternoon I helped Leah take the widow's children to a park, and we returned to find Tad loading the dishwasher. He flashed me a big smile. "As you can see, my goal is still to squeeze in as many dishes as possible. I tried to change, but it felt like I was wasting space. So there's no reason to nag me anymore when you go back to the turn of the century, right?"

"I'll try not to," I said kindly. "But couldn't you put all the plates together..."

Tad roared with laughter. "You can't help it, can you?" He grabbed my hand and twirled me around, then he gave me a big hug. "I love you, Emma. Don't ever change."

I settled into a routine of assisting Tad at the storehouse, helping Leah with the widow's children and visiting ill members of the ward. The time flew by and I soon realized I'd been in the future for nearly four months! I loved living in Zion and I had no desire to return to present day. Who could blame me? My children were already grown, I had adorable grandchildren, and I felt surrounded by love and spirituality.

I knew it couldn't last forever, though, and I prayed earnestly about the matter. I finally received the impression I should just be patient. I sensed I would soon return, but the Lord had a few things He wanted me to witness first.

I often found myself worrying about Justin, though. I couldn't decide which was better for him—to have returned to Lincoln Point or to have died in the mountains. At least if he had died maybe he'd still have a chance at salvation.

We also received a surprise visit from Tara and her parents one Sunday. She was adjusting well to just being a regular teenager, and her parents couldn't stop talking about how well-behaved she was. She had enrolled in the high school near their home and was truly enjoying life among the Saints after years of hardship in Lincoln Point.

• • • •

A big surprise came when a group of 15 people arrived on our doorstep one afternoon. I could tell they were recent arrivals by their tattered clothing and weary faces. They were of Hispanic descent, and some spoke in Spanish to each other.

I joined Tad on the porch as their elderly, stooped leader came forward. "Hello, sir. Are you Bishop Tad North?"

Tad nodded. "I am. How may I help you?"

"Elder Dalton told us to locate you when we arrived in Zion."

"Elder Dalton?" Tad asked in surprise. "You mean Doug Dalton?"

"Yes, sir," the man said. "I'm Jorge Rodriguez. Elder Dalton baptized me into the church many years ago. We saw him again in Jersey City just a few months ago, and he told us to come here and find you."

I stepped forward. "You're all welcome in our home. You're safe here." The group let out cries of gratitude.

The next week was a bit crazy as we helped the Rodriguez family get settled. Tad found them a pair of homes within our ward boundaries, and they became citizens of Zion.

I was excited they'd seen Doug, but we were so busy getting them settled that I never got to really ask them how they'd been reunited. So on the following Sunday we invited Jorge and his silver-haired wife, Yesenia, to come to dinner and tell us their story. Their names sounded so familiar to me, but I couldn't remember when Doug would've mentioned them.

The conversation at dinner was mainly small-talk, but after dinner we gathered in the family room with all of our children and grandchildren. Heather sat on the floor in front of the Rodriguezes, eager to hear what this couple would say about her father.

Jorge smiled kindly at her. "Long ago, Yesenia invited your father and his missionary companion to our home," Jorge said. "I wasn't too interested in the Mormons, but I'd been having some strange dreams."

I sat up with a start. "You're in Doug's book," I said excitedly.

Jorge nodded slightly. "Yes, Elder Dalton mentioned us in his story. So you know what I'm about to say?"

"I think so, but go ahead," I said. "Sorry to interrupt."

Jorge cleared his throat. "The first dream I had was of Joseph Smith receiving the First Vision, but it was the second dream I received that confused me. It always started with a dream in which I'm on a dark battlefield as part of an army that includes both my and Yesenia's extended family. We endure a fierce battle, and most of the relatives are nearly dead. Then I take command of the army, and I lead them to victory. We then move to a glorious city."

Jorge choked up a little, and Yesenia said, "For many years we thought the dream only symbolized when Jorge joined the church and helped our families become active members. But now it's as if the dream is being fulfilled once again, in a more literal way."

Jorge had regained his composure, and he said, "We had often talked of moving to Utah, but we were doing well in New Jersey, and we all had callings in the ward there. We moved a block from Jersey City's stake center, and life was going well.

"But when the war broke out, we were basically cut off from the rest of the church. Our home was looted, and we escaped to the stake center. A journey to Utah was now out of the question, since we didn't have any supplies or really even a map. When we prayed, we seemed guided by the Spirit to stay put, so we did. We somehow grew food in some of the classrooms from some seeds we found in the cupboards."

"What about the rest of the city's inhabitants?" Heather asked.

"Well, anyone who went outside for very long seemed to be cut down by a strange disease, or else they'd go crazy and kill each other," Yesenia said. "Then one day we could hear loud crackling and explosions coming from Manhattan. We'd barricaded the windows and doors to protect ourselves, but we opened a window and could feel an intense heat.

"All of Manhattan was engulfed in flames. Then the fire seemed to jump the river toward Jersey City and Newark. We huddled inside a bathroom and prayed as the wall of flame roared over us. The church was hardly touched, but it ruined the church's satellite dish, so we lost all outside contact. We were blessed, though. Every other building around us was destroyed."

Jorge shook his head. "After that, we were the only people still there," he said. "The fire had cleansed everything, though, and we finally felt safe to go outside. We planted a garden outside the church, hoping to eventually head west, but our wait lasted several years as we just tried to stay alive. Then Elder Dalton arrived. He was such a welcome sight!"

"How was he?" Heather asked. "I miss him so much!"

"He looked pretty healthy," Yesenia said. "He explained that he'd been called as one of the 144,000 High Priests who were scouring the earth one final time, and he told us he'd walked nearly the whole way across the country. He'd had success encouraging people to gather to Zion, but he'd felt compelled to make sure all of his friends had made it out of New Jersey. We're sure glad he stopped by."

We all laughed as she made it sound like Doug had just casually showed up for lunch. In reality, Doug had probably suffered through trials much worse than his World War II experiences.

"Elder Dalton stayed with us for two weeks as we got ready to leave, then we headed west, and he headed north to Canada," Jorge said. "It was hard to see him go off alone, but he'd told us the Lord would protect him."

"Well, we're glad you've finally made it to the glorious city!" Tad said. "We're also pleased that you'll be in our ward."

• • • •

The following morning at 6:00 a.m. the phone rang and Tad jumped out of bed to answer it. I didn't listen too closely, since I was growing accustomed to being a bishop's wife, with the phone always ringing at crazy hours. But I heard Tad conclude the call by saying, "At the temple? Yes, both Emma and I will be there, President."

That caught my attention.

As Tad hung up the phone I asked, "We're going to the temple? I don't have a recommend."

Tad crossed the room to our dresser, opened his wallet and pulled out a small card. "Are you Emma Dalton North?" he asked, reading the card.

"Of course."

"Then this is your recommend," he said.

"I see you still have to hold onto it for me so I don't lose it," I said with a grin. "How many more times have I lost my recommend over the years?"

"Just once a decade, without fail." He glanced again at the card. "You're in luck! It doesn't expire for two more months. Now let's get moving. There's a special meeting in the temple at 8:00 a.m., and the stake president made it sound urgent. We can make it in time if we catch the next bus."

Chapter Thirty-Five

My goal of entering the New Jerusalem Temple came true within an hour. We hurried inside and changed into white clothing. Tad waited for me outside the women's dressing room, then he took my hand and guided me toward the temple chapel, which was situated under the center dome. The excitement in the air was almost electrifying. Something definitely important was about to happen.

I stopped suddenly in front of a glass-enclosed room along the hall. The room was filled with dozens of sets of gold and brass plates! They were carefully arranged and glittered in the light. "Where did these come from?" I asked.

"That's the collection of plates Mormon and Moroni abridged to make the Book of Mormon," Tad said. "They were recently brought to the temple after being hidden for hundreds of years. The records of the Ten Tribes are in there, too."

I stayed riveted in place, my eyes probing the various plates. Some were quite large, yet some were the size of my hand. Tad finally grabbed my elbow. "Come on, we're going to be late," he said.

At least 20,000 people were already in the chapel. We found seats near the back of the room. I stared up at the gorgeous arched ceiling, which glistened in the morning sun. A hush fell over the crowd as an elderly man made his way to the pulpit at the far end of the immense room.

"Thank you for coming so promptly, brothers and sisters," the man said. "I hate to give you a much-needed day off, but you'll just have to live with it."

A collective nervous chuckle passed through the crowd, and I glanced at the people near me. I guessed this was a gathering of bishops, stake presidents and their wives from throughout the entire city.

"Who's the man at the pulpit?" I whispered to Tad.

"A member of the Quorum of the Twelve," Tad whispered

back, not taking his eyes off the man.

"What's his name?" I whispered, but Tad ignored me. The man adjusted the microphone, then said, "At this moment a great gathering is taking place about 80 miles to the north of us, and we've been invited to participate in this long-prophesied event. We first gathered you here so you'd be dressed in your white clothing. It's not often you see the Ancient of Days—even Father Adam."

A jolt of the Spirit raced through the room, and excited whispers filled the chapel. The man at the pulpit just chuckled and waited for the noise to die down. Then he pointed to a set of doors on the west side of the chapel. "Every bus in the city has been obtained to carry us to the great gathering," he said. "Please exit quietly, and we'll see you there."

The crowd stood as one and reverently moved to the doors. Everyone's face beamed with excitement and anticipation. I grabbed Tad's arm—apparently I was the only one who didn't understand what was going on.

"What did he mean about Father Adam?" I whispered. "Where are we going?"

Tad looked at me in surprise. "Don't you know? To Adam-ondi-Ahman."

• • • •

We became part of a 200-bus caravan that worked its way along a highway heading north. Within a few miles we left the city and passed through fruit orchards. Large red apples hung from the branches along the road, and later juicy peaches bent the tree limbs nearly to the ground.

I was still unsure where we were going. I put my mouth to Tad's ear and whispered, "What did you call this place we're headed? Andy-omdi-Dannon?"

"You're joking, right?" Tad asked.

"No! I don't understand what's happening!" I said this a little too loudly, and several fellow passengers turned to stare at me. Tad grinned painfully and waved them off.

"She's just nervous," he said. Once everyone had turned back around, Tad patted my knee and leaned toward me.

"Adam-ondi-Ahman means 'the land of God where Adam dwelt.' The prophets have taught that the Garden of Eden was located where New Jerusalem now is," Tad said softly. "When Adam and Eve were cast out of the garden, they settled in the area where we're now going. Just before he died, Adam gathered all his righteous descendants in the Valley of Adam-ondi-Ahman to bless them."

"I vaguely remember hearing about that once when somebody went off on a wild tangent during Sunday School," I said. "But what does that matter to us?"

"The Prophet Joseph taught that Adam would again visit Adam-ondi-Ahman, where he'll preside over a great council in preparation for the Second Coming. At this council, all who have held keys of priesthood authority will give an accounting to Adam of their stewardship."

"All? You mean everyone who ever was a priesthood leader?" I asked. "Like Moses and Abraham?"

"Correct," Tad said. "And then Christ will come and receive back the keys as one of the final steps to ushering in the Millennium. That's why everyone is so excited! We've been waiting for this meeting for a long time."

I still couldn't really comprehend the magnitude of what he was saying, but I knew a wonderful experience awaited us.

We passed through a community where a regal temple stood. "This is the city of Liberty," Tad told me. I spotted a visitors center on the lot next to the temple. "Is that where Liberty Jail was?" I asked.

"That's right," Tad said. "The visitors center was built over the actual spot. That's where Joseph Smith suffered for so many months."

The buses picked up speed, and soon the landscape was racing by. For the next hour we alternately passed farmland and beautiful cities. I was nearly bursting with questions, but everyone seemed to be busy praying or quickly repenting in preparation for the upcoming spiritual feast. The only sound was instrumental hymns being played over the bus stereo system.

As the last city faded behind us, our bus came to a stop at the edge of the road alongside a beautiful meadow. Further beyond were rolling hills covered with lush grasses and beautiful flowers. Tad took my hand and we quietly joined thousands of others walking up the road. We walked for about a half-mile before cresting a hill, and my eyes could barely focus as I beheld an endless throng of white-robed souls gathered in a long, sloping valley. A beautiful river flowed beneath the bluffs on the valley's far side, and every available inch of the hillside was covered with people. I couldn't even see the end of the crowd. "There must be a million people here," I said.

"There's probably many more than that," Tad said.

A long wooden structure had been erected at one end of the valley, and many dignified men in holy robes sat there. A spot for our group had been saved near the front, and we were kindly greeted by the angelic crowds who parted to let us pass by.

"Wow, why do we get the best seats?" I whispered.

"Because we're mortals," Tad said patiently. "Our eyes and ears don't work as well as the rest of the people here." He motioned to the crowds behind us.

"Are you saying they're..."

"Yes, resurrected beings," Tad whispered. "Now please hold your questions."

Wooden benches awaited us. I supposed resurrected beings could stand all day if required, but we mortals needed a place to sit. Tad guided me to a bench about 30 yards from the stage, and I let myself be absorbed by the incredible spirit that surrounded the place. I felt as if I could float.

Once we mortals were seated, an angelic choir on the valley's north side began to sing the hymn "Adam-ondi-Ahman," which fit the occasion perfectly. In crystal-clear harmony the choir sang:

> *The earth was once a garden place,*
> *with all her glories common,*
> *And men did live a holy race,*
> *and worship Jesus face to face,*
> *In Adam-ondi-Ahman.*
> *We read that Enoch walked with God,*
> *above the power of mammon,*
> *While Zion spread herself abroad,*
> *and Saints and angels sang aloud,*
> *In Adam-ondi-Ahman.*
> *Her land was good and greatly blessed,*
> *beyond all Israel's Canaan,*
> *Her fame was known from east to west,*
> *her peace was great, and pure the rest,*

Of Adam-ondi-Ahman.

Then an indescribable sensation passed through my body as the entire valley joined in the final verse. The ground seemed to shake as the vast congregation sang:

Hosanna to such days to come,
the Savior's second coming,
When all the earth in glorious bloom
affords the Saints a holy home,
Like Adam-ondi-Ahman.

A heavenly peace settled on the valley as the song's words faded away. I watched the pulpit expectantly. A large, muscular man with white hair sat in the center chair, and I knew instantly that he was Adam. At his left was a stunningly beautiful woman who radiated joy—Eve, the mother of the human race.

Sitting at Adam's right hand was a man who could've been Adam's twin. This man stood and walked to the podium.

"That must be Seth," Tad whispered. "The scriptures say he looked just like his father, and he really does." I looked back and forth between the two men, and it was like seeing double.

There wasn't a microphone, but Seth's voice carried across the acoustically perfect valley. "Welcome to this great gathering," Seth said. "Father Adam presides here today, and he has asked that I conduct this meeting."

He explained the purpose of the meeting, which was to return the keys of each gospel dispensation back to Adam, who then would return them to the Savior himself in preparation for the Lord's millennial reign. To say the least, I was blown away to be there, especially when Noah—yes, *that* Noah— offered the opening prayer, pleading that we would do the Lord's will that day.

I scanned the crowd, and I sensed a great order in our seating. We were arranged by dispensations, with the priesthood leaders of the First Dispensation—which began 6,000 years ago when Adam and Eve left the Garden—standing on the left hillside. Then the dispensations circled around the valley, and on the hillside to my right were priesthood leaders I recognized from our dispensation, which began with Joseph Smith. The odd thing is these men all appeared to be in their late-20s or mid-30s. I spotted Spencer W. Kimball with dark hair, and Joseph F. Smith looked almost the same as when I'd met him in 1868.

I pointed them out to Tad and asked, "How come they're

resurrected already?"

Tad shrugged. "Once a person can do more for the kingdom with his body than he can without it, the Lord will resurrect him. I believe it is pretty rare, though, for someone from our dispensation. I'd say the only ones from our dispensation who've been resurrected are the people on that hillside."

It was a day filled with priesthood ordinances and ceremonies as the keys of the kingdom were returned to the Earth's first patriarch. The Spirit was very strong, and I soaked everything in. It didn't dawn on me until afterward, but the meeting seemed to take place in another language. I only say that because although I understood everything that was said, my mind can only recall the meanings. I believe that during the meeting we mortals received the gift of tongues so that we could understand the language of Adam. Or better said, we heard the language of heaven—a language we'd known once before.

I was so enraptured in the events taking place that I never got tired of sitting on that wooden bench, and I was stunned when Tad told me nine hours had passed. It had seemed like only minutes! The sun was creeping toward the western horizon as the transfer of priesthood power was completed. Adam stood before us and wept openly. "The time is at hand, dear Lord," he prayed. "We have done what thou asked us to do."

He stood silently, then the most glorious being I've ever seen appeared at Adam's side. We mortals gasped in surprise and awe, while the others in the crowd bowed in reverence before the Lord Jesus Christ, the Savior of the world. We quickly followed their example once we regained our composure.

"I accept your offerings," the Savior said in a smooth, penetrating voice. His voice soothed my soul. I lifted my eyes to see Him, and tears rolled down my face. Every wicked act I'd ever done crossed my mind, and I lowered my head in shame. Yet I also felt elevated, knowing that through the Savior's sacrifice and by living the best I knew how, I could return someday to my heavenly home.

The rights and privileges of the priesthood were returned to the Savior, the rightful heir. He then spoke to us, and I felt my heart would burst with joy to hear His glorious words as He described the great Millennial era that would soon come.

Abraham gave the closing prayer, then we mortals were instructed to return to our homes. We were emotionally and physically drained, and I stayed sitting on the bench as the crowd began to disperse.

I felt a hand on my shoulder, and turned to look into the playful ice-blue eyes of an old friend. "Sister Emma, are you still traveling around?" a beardless Brigham Young asked.

I leapt to my feet and gave him a hug, but I quickly stepped back. "Oh sorry, you're resurrected and all..."

Brigham laughed. "It's OK to touch me. I'm flesh and bones just like you."

I examined his face, which was youthful and wrinkle-free. "Wow, I can't wait to be resurrected if it improves things this well. You look so much better than you used to."

"Well, thanks a lot!" Brigham said jokingly. Tad was standing nervously nearby, and Brigham turned to him. "You must be Tad, the man with enough faith to marry a girl who tells outlandish tales."

Tad stepped forward and shook Brigham's hand. "It took me a while to believe her," Tad said bashfully.

"I know what you mean," Brigham said. "I had the same problem in 1868."

A regal-looking couple in holy robes passed within a few yards of us, and my jaw dropped. "Is that Joseph and Emma Smith?"

"It certainly is," Brigham said. "Would you like to meet them?"

"Um, do you and Emma get along now?" I asked.

Brigham crinkled his brow in confusion, then he laughed. "Oh, we patched up our differences ages ago."

Brigham called to them and they walked toward us. Tad and I were speechless, but Emma took my hand and said, "You're such a pretty girl. What is your name?"

"I'm Emma. My parents named me after you," I said breathlessly. "It's a great privilege to meet you."

She smiled appreciatively. Brigham took a moment to explain my time-travels to the Smiths, and they nodded in understanding. "So you'll be returning to the past, I suppose?" Emma asked.

"I think so, but I don't know when," I said. "I'm really enjoying living in Zion."

I paused to shake Joseph's hand. His eyes radiated perfect

happiness, and I knew I was meeting one of the greatest men of all time.

"It's a pleasure to meet you, Sister Emma," Joseph said. "It sounds like you've been busy serving in the kingdom."

"It is nothing compared to what you did," I said. "You and Emma sacrificed so much."

Joseph smiled. "We've been rewarded much more than we could've ever imagined. Keep the faith, dear sister."

The Smiths waved good-bye and wished me luck, then I gave Brigham one final hug before Tad and I slowly walked up the slope toward the bus. We were too overwhelmed to even speak. I'd just had the highlight of my life, and I figured nothing would ever top that.

I was wrong.

"Emma," a wondrous voice said. I turned to see the Savior standing five feet away. I immediately fell to my knees, as did everyone around me. I felt Him approach, and I saw the nail marks in his feet as he neared me. He took my hand and lifted me to my feet. "Oh, dear Savior," I said. "I'm not worthy to be in your presence."

He smiled kindly. "You underestimate your value, my dear one. I've come to thank you for the errands you've performed in my behalf."

I blushed and stared at the ground. "It was nothing, really."

"Someday you'll see the full extent of your good works," the Savior said. I looked at His radiant face. His blue eyes were as deep as eternity.

"You shall soon return to your proper time, and you'll never again be called on such an errand. Once you return, your family must be your top priority."

"I understand, dear Savior," I said softly.

"But I must ask one more thing of you before you go back," the Savior said. "Please return to Provo and assist your parents for a short time. They are growing older and need your aid right now."

"Certainly."

"Thank you. Mathoni will again be your guide," Jesus said. "You have been a good and faithful servant." He put His hand to my cheek, then vanished before our eyes.

Chapter Thirty-Six

We walked in silent wonderment to the buses. "This has been a day beyond compare," Tad finally said. "It's like getting a taste of heaven."

I nodded as we found our bus. "I can't wait to tell the kids."

Then I stopped in shock. A blue Nissan was parked beside our bus, with a white-robed Mathoni leaning against the hood.

"Do we have to go now?" I asked Mathoni. "Can't I see the kids once more?"

"Sorry, but I've been instructed to get you to Provo by sunrise," Mathoni said. "This is going to take some fancy driving, even by my standards. I've got a change of clothes for you in the car."

I felt such a letdown, and I instinctively clutched onto Tad. "I'm not ready to leave," I said fiercely.

Tad hugged me as Mathoni watched sympathetically. "Don't forget, the sooner you complete your errand, the sooner the 'older Emma' can return," Tad said. "You'll be here for all the excitement of the Millennium. Now go back and make sure the 'younger Tad' stays active in the church. You're the spiritual giant in the family, not me."

I clutched him tightly and gave him a kiss. "You're wonderful. Tell the kids I'll see them soon."

We walked swiftly to the car and I climbed in. Mathoni took a moment to shake hands with Tad, then he got behind the wheel and started the engine. "Be prepared for the ride of your life," he said as he swung the car around.

Mathoni floored the gas pedal and we shot forward like a rocket. I dug the fingernails of my left hand into Mathoni's right arm. "Slow down!"

"Sorry, but no," he said with a smile. "By the way, I can't feel physical pain, so your fingernails aren't doing any good. But please let go so I can steer. I'd hate to crash—for your sake."

• • • •

We were going so fast that it seemed we were actually chasing the sun on its westward course for a while, but eventually darkness came upon us and the long day caught up with me. I slept soundly, but I awoke briefly for a bathroom break during a brief stop at Mathoni's gasoline stash near Grand Junction. Then the next thing I remember is pulling off the freeway into downtown Provo. It was depressing to return to a dilapidated Utah Valley after having lived in New Jerusalem.

"Hello, sleepyhead," Mathoni said. "Yesterday seemed to wear you out."

Within ten minutes Mathoni pulled up in front of the temple gates. I was glad to see The Mighty One's band had returned to Lincoln Point without damaging BYU or the temple.

"Let them know I'll be back in an hour," Mathoni said.

"Aren't you coming in?" I asked.

He tapped the car's fuel gauge. "I've got to go fill the tank on this gas guzzler and check the oil," he said. "I've got another supply of fuel hidden in Pleasant Grove."

"OK, I'll tell them," I said, not sure why they'd need to know. "Thanks again."

Mathoni pulled away, and one of the temple brethren opened the gate for me. "It's good to see you again," the man said. "How are things in Zion?"

"Wonderful," I said. "I hated to leave."

He began relocking the gate, and I hurried up the sidewalk to the temple entrance. I entered the lobby and saw a thin, balding middle-aged man speaking to a gathering of people. "And so I got out of Detroit and into a pond before the pack of dogs caught up with me," he told the group. "The water smelled so bad..."

The man's words faded away, then he leaped over a sofa, wrapped his arms around my waist and twirled me through the air. "Doug?" I asked in surprise. "Is it really you?"

Doug put me down and smiled widely. "Emma, you're sure a beautiful sight! Mom and Dad told me how you saved my kids."

I cringed. "I failed, though. Justin ran away and returned to Lincoln Point."

"What?" Doug asked in dismay. "When did this happen?"

"On our way to New Jerusalem," I said nervously.

Doug's face relaxed. "Whew, you scared me. Justin's here! I saw him just a few minutes ago!"

"He came back here? I didn't know that!"

We quickly began a search for Justin and found him reading a book in the basement. He couldn't figure out the reason for the commotion until he spotted me.

"Oh, hello there, Eddie," he said in shock. "I was hoping to see you again someday so I could apologize for how I acted. I was a fool to try driving the car."

"Apology accepted, but I don't understand why you're here. Didn't you go back to Lincoln Point?"

He shook his head. "I fully intended to, but a day after leaving you I was dying from thirst. I'd worn myself out climbing out of the mountains the previous day, and now I was in the middle of a scorching desert and was losing strength rapidly. I realized what a fool I'd been, and now it was too late. I curled up in a ball and awaited my fate. Then in desperation I began to pray. I prayed for forgiveness for my sins rather than to be rescued, since survival seemed out of the question."

"Then how did you make it back here?"

"Just as I was about to lose consciousness, a man picked me off the ground and carried me up a mountainside," Justin said humbly. "The man found a small spring and helped me get a drink. He pointed out some berries nearby, and then he gave me directions to a small canyon on the next mountain where grapes and apples grew. He turned to leave, but I cried out and asked him to save my sister. He said, 'She and her companions are already safe in New Jerusalem.' Then he disappeared."

"Yes, a man named Mathoni helped us get the car out of the ravine," I said. "He's one of the Savior's disciples."

Justin nodded. "After he disappeared I knew I'd seen an angel or something. I was glad I was alive, but then the torment set in as I realized what I'd given up. It took me a full week to get back to Provo, and all I wanted to do was see my grandparents."

Mom put her hand on Justin's shoulder. "He came back a changed person. He's been so helpful and cooperative."

"I finally found out what is really important," Justin said softly.

"There's one more little surprise," Doug said. "This woman's nickname is indeed Eddie, but she is really Emma, my big sister. She traveled through time to save you at Lincoln Point."

Justin's jaw dropped. "You're my aunt? Why didn't you just tell me in the first place?"

I shook my head. "You would've treated me just like you treated Heather. It worked out best this way, and I'm so glad to see you've become a new person."

Dad then corralled us all into one big hug. "It's been a long time since we've had both children together," Mom said happily. "Emma, I'm so glad you made it back in time to see Doug and Justin. They're leaving for Zion today."

"It will be a wonderful time to arrive," I said. "Yesterday was the great meeting at Adam-ondi-Ahman."

The group broke into gasps and small cheers. "The meeting at Adam-ondi-Ahman has already happened?" Dad asked in awe. "The Second Coming is very near."

Doug frowned. "Maybe I shouldn't even try to get to Zion," he said. "I'd rather be here than out in the desert when the Second Coming arrives."

"You don't have to worry," I said happily. "Mathoni drove me here, and he said he'd be back in an hour. I'm sure he intends to give you a ride to Zion."

"That would be wonderful," Doug said. "I can't wait to see Heather."

"Let's get you all some breakfast then," Mom said.

"You're always watching out for your kids, aren't you?" I asked.

She clutched my arm. "Always."

• • • •

We went to the temple cafeteria and took a table together. Once we were all eating I told Doug, "I read your book. You're a better writer than you ever let on."

"I was just trying to write half as well as you," he said humbly.

"I really enjoyed it," I said. "But how did you get back together with Becky?"

Doug became thoughtful, and Mom and Dad chuckled. "That was a miracle in itself," Dad said. "Doug didn't react very well to getting spurned."

"What do you mean?" I asked.

"Well, it all started when someone told Chris Taggart that Doug was writing rude things about him," Mom said.

"You weren't too rude," I said. "Wasn't Tex the one who called him a beanpole?"

"Technically," Doug said. "Anyway, Chris hunted me down at school and we had a small confrontation in the Kimball Tower. I told him to get a life, and he took a swing at me. I ducked, and he broke his hand against the wall."

"Oh, no!" I said in horror. "That probably didn't help his basketball career."

"You're right," Doug said. "He was never the same player after that, but the injury made Becky became even more attached to him as she nursed him back to health."

"That's the second time an injury cost Doug a girl," Dad said with a chuckle. "First Ingrid fell for a wounded Tex, and then Becky fell for Chris."

"It must be in their genes," Doug muttered.

"I'm confused," I said. "You did end up getting married to Becky, right?"

"Thankfully yes, but it took a long time," Doug said." After several months I got a letter from Becky. She was in the MTC!"

"Wow! What happened with Mr. Beanpole?"

"Becky discovered he wasn't much fun to be around when he wasn't the center of attention," Doug said with a roll of his eyes. "Chris did eventually get an offer to play basketball in Europe, though, but he didn't even tell Becky he was leaving! He broke off their engagement by sending her a postcard."

"What an idiot!" I said. "So that's when Becky decided to serve a mission?"

Doug nodded. "She served in the Canary Islands and returned home a calmer, more unselfish person. And she was even more beautiful. I only had a year left of school when she got back, and we immediately hooked up again. In fact, you two became close friends—almost like sisters."

"That's wonderful," I said. "I'm eager to meet her."

Someone cleared his throat near the cafeteria entrance, and we turned to see Mathoni standing there.

Justin jumped out of his chair. "Hey, that's the guy who saved me in the desert!"

"That's Mathoni," I said, waving to him. "He specializes in saving people."

Mathoni walked over to us and put his hand on Justin's shoulder. "I'm glad to see you made it here all right. Any side effects from those wild berries?"

"No, I'm fine," Justin said.

"I'm happy to hear it," Mathoni said. Then he turned to Doug. "Elder Dalton, would you and your son like to drive back to New Jerusalem? I've had an urgent matter come up, but feel free to take the car."

"That's very kind of you," Doug said. "We'll gladly take your offer. You've probably got a million things to do in the next few days."

"You're not far off," Mathoni said. "I think we're down to crunch time. In fact, I recommend you two leave immediately. I'll catch up with you near Grand Junction to help you refuel."

I smiled at Mathoni. "You must be excited," I said. "You'll soon see your wife and daughters again."

Mathoni grinned from ear to ear. "I'm getting pretty antsy. It will be a wonderful reunion. See you soon." He waved and headed to the doorway, but I swear he vanished before he left the room.

"That's an amazing man," Dad said. "He's helped us more than we'll ever know."

Mom then held out her arms to her son and grandson, who warmly embraced her. "you'd better heed Mathoni's advice and leave now," Mom said. "Let's get you packed."

We returned to the main floor and helped load the car, which was waiting at the front entrance. I went down the hill to unlock the gate, and Doug and Justin drove away to reunite with the rest of the family. As I relocked the gate I glimpsed four people struggling up the hill about 100 yards away. They looked muddy and straggly, and I checked to make sure I'd turned the electric fence back on. I was ready to return to the temple when the sunlight hit one person's hair just right. A purple glint was clearly visible.

"Devri, is that you?" I shouted.

My purple-haired friend raised her hand. "Who's there?" the girl called back. "Is that you, Heather?" It was Devri! Her hair must've made a complete cycle through the rainbow.

I waved my arm. "No it's Em...I mean Eddie! I'll let you in!"

Within a minute Devri and three other girls I'd met at the Lincoln Point hideout were giving me hugs. "What brings you here?" I asked.

"I just felt it was time to get out of that place," Devri said. "We've done all we could. After you escaped, Mo became even more depraved. I don't think anyone there has a shred of decency left."

"I think we can find a place for you here," I said. "I'm so happy to see you again."

Boom! A huge lightning bolt split the western sky, and the resulting thunderclap knocked us all to the ground. I got to my knees to see a mile-wide pillar of black smoke rise from West Mountain. Huge flames shot upward and consumed every building along its northern foothills. We watched in amazement for five minutes, and soon there was nothing left of Lincoln Point but smoke and ashes.

The girls were crying and shaking, and I helped them calm down as we finally started walking to the temple. "That could've been us," Devri said in a stunned voice.

"Maybe you were the only reason it didn't get burned before," I said. "The Lord was probably just waiting for the last good people to leave the city."

She merely nodded, and we were soon greeted by all the temple workers, who were outside watching the city burn. Mom and Dad saw me and hurried to my side. I introduced the girls, and soon they were being taken care of by the female temple workers.

"I'm so glad you got the kids out of that wicked place," Mom quietly said to me. "I knew the Lord wouldn't let it last much longer."

I joined the girls in the women's dressing room, where they'd been able to shower and had received new clothing. Devri smiled at me and gave me a hug. "I'm glad you also made it out of there alive," she said. "Did Tara ever find her parents?"

I nodded happily. "Yes, they greeted her with open arms."

I led the girls downstairs to the living quarters, where I saw Mom and Dad gathered around a TV with other temple workers. Everyone was excitedly milling around, and Brother Newman passed by us, seeming very upset.

"What's going on?" I asked him.

"There are reports out of Jerusalem that the two apostles were killed last night," Brother Newman said. "Their bodies are lying in the street."

"How horrible," I said. "What does that mean?"

"That the Second Coming is imminent," Brother Newman said hastily.

"How do you know that?" I asked in surprise.

He gave me an irritated look. "The scriptures say the two apostles will rise on the third day, and then the Savior will return. It also means Angie is going to lose her soul!"

Brother Newman hung his head in anguish, then a stricken look came across his face as he clutched his chest and slumped to the ground.

"Brother Newman!" I screamed. Mom and Dad rushed to us and began performing CPR on him, while other brethren gave Brother Newman a blessing. But it was as if his spirit had slipped away and wasn't going to return. After five minutes there still wasn't a pulse.

"Let him go," Dad finally said quietly.

But then Brother Newman stirred briefly and looked my father in the eyes.

"Tell Angie I'm gone," he groaned. Then he departed this life.

Chapter Thirty-Seven

Brother Newman's body was taken into a side room, and a lady who'd once worked for a mortician began preparing the body for burial. The rest of us gathered for an impromptu meeting in the temple lobby.

"It seems like we came at the wrong time," Devri told me.

I put my arm around her and peered out the front window at the smoking remains of Lincoln Point. "Believe me, you came just in time."

Dad stood before the group. He was still pale from the unexpected turn of events, and his age was starting to show as he rested both hands on a chair. After a brief explanation of Brother Newman's death, Dad said, "As you know, Brother Newman's last words to me were, 'Tell Angie I'm gone.' I will honor that request."

Cries of dismay arose from the group, including from me. "I'll go tell her," I called out. "I know where she is."

Dad waved a hand in dismissal. "If any of those helmeted thugs from Lincoln Point survived the burning of their city, they'd chop you into pieces."

He was right. A man standing near me raised his hand. "I'll go, Brother Dalton."

Dad shook his head. "I've known Angie since she was a teenager, and I'm going to ask her to come to her father's funeral. She probably won't, but I need to try. Besides, if I get killed somehow, the Second Coming isn't too far off. I wouldn't mind being a tourist in the spirit world for a little while."

Dad's off-beat comment lightened the tension in the room. Mom looked at me and shrugged. "What can it hurt?" she whispered. "This could be Angie's last chance."

Dad looked around the room, and no one spoke. "Well, get my bike out of the storage so I can go," he said. "Also, I feel Brother Newman deserves a proper burial."

Another man spoke up. "Where should we bury him? Here on the temple grounds?"

Dad frowned, deep in thought. "No, he should be buried next to his sweet wife Flora, over in the Evergreen Cemetery. I'll call Jason at Thanksgiving Point and arrange to have the train pick up the body tomorrow at 9:00 a.m. I'll need two or three men to come along to help dig the grave. Michelle and Emma, I'd like you to go with them. I'll meet you at Springville's Center Street Depot at 10 a.m., hopefully with Angie at my side."

$$\bullet \quad \bullet \quad \bullet \quad \bullet$$

I spent the evening talking with Devri, who was very curious about the temple and what we believed. She wanted to see the upper floors of the temple, but I explained that only worthy church members could go there. "And usually, even the basement is only for church members, but these are unusual times," I said. "When I get back from the cemetery, I'll tell you all about our beliefs. I think you'll like them."

Several female temple workers helped arrange a room for the girls to sleep in. I checked on the girls 20 minutes later, and they had already drifted off to sleep.

I didn't sleep too well, however, knowing my aging father was somewhere alone on the streets of Springville. But he was cautious, and I felt he'd find Angie. I had serious doubts about "Serena the High Priestess" giving a hoot about her father's death, though.

Jason and his crew arrived promptly at 9:00 a.m., and they loaded Brother Newman's hastily-made casket into the caboose. The train crew had traded the usual boxcar for a passenger car, and our small group was instinctively quiet as we got on board and headed south. I peered out the window, and smoke from the destruction of Lincoln Point filled the morning air. I shuddered to think of the lost generation I'd encountered in that evil place. It was a relief to know it was destroyed.

As we approached Springville, my anxiety began to build. Would Dad be there? The train began slowing down, and I moved to the eastern window. My heart jumped at seeing Dad and Angie standing at the Center Street depot.

Dad pulled open the door and climbed in, but Angie stood defiantly outside. "I don't see a casket, Mr. Dalton!" she said defiantly. "Where is he? Is this some sort of trick?"

"The casket must be in the caboose," Dad said.

"I told you I'm not going to the cemetery," Angie said angrily.

Mom moved to the doorway. "Hello, Angie."

"My name's Serena, old woman," my former friend sneered. Then she softened slightly. "Hey, aren't you Mrs. Dalton?"

"I am," Mom said softly. "It's been a long time, hasn't it?"

"It sure has," Serena said. "What ever happened to your daughter Emma?"

"She's here in the train," Mom said. "Come on in. She'd love to see you."

I stiffened. The last thing I wanted to do was speak with Serena.

"Self-righteous Emma is on board?" Serena asked. "This is a face I'd like to see."

Serena climbed aboard, and Ron didn't hesitate in getting the train rolling. Serena didn't even seem to notice the train lurch forward as she searched everyone's faces. Finally she stopped at mine. I could only hope she'd been too drunk during our earlier confrontation to remember me. I was in luck.

"Holy Moses! Look at that face," Serena said in shock. "You Mormons must have an army of plastic surgeons to keep everyone looking so young."

I smiled. "Thanks for the compliment. But this face isn't the work of a plastic surgeon. I owe it all to clean living."

That was the wrong thing to say. "You little know-it-all," Serena shrieked. "Even now, you still think you're better than me." She lunged at my throat, but several of the brethren pulled her off me and pinned her to the floor.

"Angie, Serena—whoever you are—I never meant to act better than you," I said in despair.

"Then how come you quit coming to the dances with us?" Serena asked. "You wouldn't even return my phone calls."

I stared at her silently, finally realizing how much our friendship had meant to her. I could now see I'd deeply hurt her.

"I always liked you," I said with tears in my eyes. "But it was the sensual atmosphere I didn't like, and the type of guys you wanted to hang out with, you know?"

Serena's eyes never softened. "Nice try, Emma, but your explanation is a few decades too late." She fought her way off the floor. "I want to see my father," she said, pushing her elderly captors to the side.

Dad opened the doors between the passenger car and the caboose, and Serena stepped into the other car, giving me a vulgar gesture as she exited. I just hung my head and cried.

• • • •

Within minutes the train stopped directly west of the Evergreen Cemetery, and Jason and his crew unloaded the casket onto a handcart. I stayed clear of Serena, but she ignored me now and walked solemnly alongside the casket, finally acting like a dutiful daughter after all these years.

Flora Newman had been buried in one of the newest sections of the cemetery, which meant we had a long uphill walk ahead of us. We slowly progressed up the cemetery's center road, and I glanced toward Grandpa Keith and Grandma Rosalie's headstone, but the grass was too tall and unkempt to see it. Only the tallest headstones could be seen. I also realized all the cemetery's trees had been chopped down, probably for firewood. Stumps stood where beautiful trees had given shade for centuries.

Mom came to my side. "Grandpa Jack and Grandma Sheila are buried near the other Daltons," she said. "Becky and Daniel are buried about 50 yards further east."

We finally reached 400 East and crossed into the new part of the cemetery. The Veterans Memorial still stood, and a few remaining strips of an American flag miraculously still flew. A few of the men had taken shovels from the train and had gone ahead of us. I now saw them digging a grave in the northeast corner of the cemetery, an area I didn't recall being used yet for burials. Now this section was filled with headstones of all shapes and sizes. I noticed that the most recent burials had homemade headstones. The last manufactured headstone had been placed several years before.

"People couldn't afford fancy headstones anymore," Mom said in reply to my unasked question.

When we finally arrived at the gravesite, the men had made a good-sized hole. The soil was sandy, which made the digging easier. Jason and his crew took over for them and they soon had the grave three feet deep in about ten minutes.

Dad inspected the hole and said, "That should be deep enough for this righteous servant of the Lord. He won't be down there long. Few men have followed the Savior as faithfully as Brother Newman did. He'll certainly be called forth in the morning of the First Resurrection."

I saw Serena roll her eyes, then she stepped forward. "I'd like to say a few words. My father always showed concern for me, but he was misguided. You're also misguided, Mr. Dalton, if you think my father's dead body will ever do anything but crumble to dust. You're all a bunch of fools."

She stepped back, and my father grinned as he said, "Thank you for your opinion, Serena. I'm sure your father is happy you are here today to honor him. Let's move forward with our business here."

The casket was carefully lowered into the hole, and the brethren quickly put the sandy soil back in place. Dad explained he would offer a dedicatory prayer on Brother Eastman's grave, but Serena interrupted him. "I'd like to go first, if you don't mind," she said.

Dad nodded, and Serena knelt at the foot of the grave. She pulled a handful of flower petals from her dress pocket and began tossing them in the air in some sort of ritual. I was eager to see how she'd end the ritual, but Serena was quickly forgotten as a circle of blazing light pierced the eastern sky above the mouth of Hobble Creek Canyon. The glorious light rapidly spread to the western horizon, and it seemed as if the heavens were unrolling like a scroll. In a manner that I can't explain, everyone on earth saw the same event I did at that moment.

The Second Coming of Jesus Christ.

Chapter Thirty-Eight

I looked into the sky and saw the Savior of the World. He was surrounded by countless numbers of angels. Then I felt myself being lifted into the air. Mom was at my side, and we clasped hands in wonderment. We saw Dad nearby and waved to him. Angels filled the sky around us, and we hovered hundreds of yards above the earth as a wall of fire roared across the earth's surface. I saw Maple Mountain seemingly melt into the flames.

Dad somehow made his way over to us. The fire's roar was deafening, but we seemed protected from the heat.

"What's happening?" I shouted to Dad.

"The earth is being cleansed by fire to usher in the Millennium!"

"I can't believe we lived to see this day," Mom called out.

We stayed suspended in the air for a few more minutes, then the flames faded away. We felt ourselves slowly returning to earth.

My thoughts returned to Angie. I hadn't seen her in the air, and my worst fears were confirmed as we landed on solid ground again. At the foot of Brother Newman's grave was a round pile of charred ashes.

"Oh, Angie," I sobbed. "I'm so sorry."

Mom and Dad comforted me, but then we began to notice a change in our surroundings as the smoke dissipated. We beheld a glorious new world! All things that were of a foul or evil nature had been consumed by the flames, and the beautiful things of the earth had been restored. The weeds and tall grass of the cemetery had been replaced with lush green grass that looked freshly mowed. The cemetery trees had also somehow returned.

The mountains had become smooth, and to the north I saw that the highest point in the valley was now the Provo Temple, which rested atop a large hill. I was pleased to see Utah Lake had miraculously filled again, and its blue waters sparkled. Another curiosity caught my eye. West Mountain had been replaced by a flower-covered meadow, with no sign of the blackened hillside that'd once been Lincoln Point.

One more surprise greeted us as a bright light streaked across the eastern sky. The earth jolted a little as it sank below the horizon. "That thing hit the earth," I cried out.

"That must be Enoch's city that was taken from the earth before the flood," Dad exclaimed. "It has returned to join with New Jerusalem!"

We began walking back toward the train in wonderment at what lay ahead in this new era. A feeling of euphoria covered the earth, and I felt rejuvenated. The Savior had finally come!

• • • •

As we walked through the older part of the cemetery, men in white robes began appearing among the headstones.

"Did those people just get resurrected?" I asked.

"Maybe, but I think they're here to help resurrect their relatives," Dad said.

"What do you mean?" I asked. "I figured the ground would just split open all throughout the cemetery so people could rise from their graves."

Dad laughed. "I'm not quite sure what's going on. Let's get down to the Dalton plot and maybe we'll get to see for ourselves."

We arrived at the Dalton family plot, but there wasn't any activity there yet. Then a white-robed man appeared before us. "Oh, hello," he said. "I didn't expect any mortals to be here. Mark and Michelle, how did you know when to be here?"

"We just happened to be at a funeral," Dad answered as he peered closely at the glorified man. "Are you Robert Dalton?"

"Yes, I am," the man said with a pleased grin. "And hello, Emma. I'm your great-great grandpa."

I cautiously took his extended hand and felt a surge of energy pass between us. "You're Keith's father, right?" I asked.

"Yes, so it's my privilege to take part in his resurrection," Robert said.

"It's an...act?" I asked.

"A resurrection is actually a priesthood ordinance," he said with a smile. "Just watch. It'll make more sense to see it done."

Robert stood at the east edge of Keith's grave and called

Keith by name, then pronounced a prayer that sounded similar to a healing blessing. Then we all stepped back as the ground near Keith's headstone began to rumble a little. Suddenly a body began to materialize up through the grass!

"Immortal bodies can pass through any earthly material," Dad whispered reverently. "There's no need to throw the dirt around and make a big mess."

I recognized Grandpa Keith's face from old family photos. His body was soon completely free from the ground, and he opened his eyes and stretched his arms above his head as if he was waking from a long nap.

"It always takes a second to get the joints moving again," Robert said happily. He stepped forward and offered Keith his hand. "How are you feeling, son?"

Keith smiled. "I've never felt better."

Robert pulled him to his feet, and Keith approached us. "It's nice to have you three here," he said as he continued to stretch his legs and swivel his arms. "Wow, this resurrected body is fantastic!" He checked his chest where the tires of a logging truck had crushed him in 1951. "I'm as good as new," he said happily. "You'll love it when it's your turn, Mark."

"I can't wait," Dad said. "My old body is getting worn out. I've still got several years until I turn 100, though. Then I'll just get changed in a twinkling of an eye."

"It's worth the wait," Keith said. "How's Doug doing? Did he get back to New Jerusalem?"

"He should've made it there yesterday," Mom said. "He was eager to see the rest of the family."

Keith smiled. "I can't wait to tease him a little. I kept waiting for him or Tex to show up in that French hospital in 1945, but he'd ditched me and gone back to his proper time."

"Thank you for helping him during his mission in New Jersey," Mom said. "That meant a great deal to all of us."

Keith chuckled a little. "I wasn't supposed to pass through the veil, but I was so proud of him that night that I slipped through and gave him a pat on the shoulder. I'm glad he sensed my presence. He's such a good man."

Robert stepped forward and motioned to the ground, and Keith slapped his forehead. "Look at me! I'm jabbering away while Rosalie is waiting impatiently on the other side of the veil. Please excuse me a moment."

It was a strange, happy feeling to talk to these men. Neither I nor my parents had ever met Robert or Keith during mortality, but we all knew each other immediately. I sensed we'd been close friends in the premortal world, and they'd been watching and helping us from the spirit world.

Keith performed the ordinance, and soon we saw Grandma Rosalie emerge through the grass. She seemed more awake than Keith had been, and she immediately put a hand to her hair as she sat up and modestly smoothed out her white robe.

"Oh, I don't have dirt in my hair, do I?" she asked.

"No, you look fine, dear," Keith said. "You passed right through the soil."

"I'm glad I only have to do that once," she said. Then Keith swept her off the ground and put her on her feet. She looked at me and said, "Hello there, Emma! How's your errand going?"

"It just keeps getting better," I said, giving her a hug. "You look splendid, Grandma." I noticed her hair was the reddish blonde of her youth. "I guess you aren't required to have white hair," Dad said. Robert's hair was flecked with gray, but Keith's was dark brown. "Nope, whatever feels best," Robert said.

"It's strange to realize you're my grandparents," Dad said. "You look fifty years younger than me!"

"You'll get your turn to be young again," Grandma Rosalie said. "Besides, it doesn't look like I gained any height," she said as she stood on her tippy-toes. "I'm still the shortest one!"

Our conversation was cut short as heavenly beings began appearing all around us. We were quickly encircled by 10 other people. It was incredible! One of the men on the far side said, "How's everything going, Robert? We got finished in Charleston and thought we'd see if you've found everyone you needed to."

"I still need to visit the Provo Cemetery to raise up my son LaVar," Robert said, "but there's someone here I think you and George will be eager to see. Emma's here."

"Mark's daughter? You're kidding me!" The man broke through the group and our eyes met. "Finity!" I exclaimed, and we clutched each other in excitement.

He kissed my cheek and asked, "Will you ever get to just stay in your own time?"

"The Lord told me that this is my final time-travel journey,"

I said. "Then I can settle down."

He laughed. "You'll hardly be settling down. You've got a busy life ahead of you."

"Thanks for believing me when I stayed with you," I said.

"I was a bit hard-headed," Finity said. "It took a few days for your story to sink in. You really made my head hurt when you talked about the future. Of course, now I could make your head spin with what I know."

"Oh, don't tell me," I pleaded. "I've absorbed too much already."

Another man stepped between us. "Sorry, Dad," he said. "You're hogging her all to yourself." He took my hand and asked, "Do you remember me, Emma?"

"Certainly, George," I said happily. "In fact, I only recently found out how you'd died. Getting killed by a lightning bolt must've been dreadful!"

George shrugged. "Oh, it really burned for a second, but my spirit left my body so fast that it hardly even hurt."

"I'm glad to hear that," I said.

We chatted for several more minutes, and in the meantime Keith resurrected Grandpa Jack, who then called forth Grandma Sheila. Talk about a family reunion!

Finity soon said it was time to move to other cemeteries, but I asked my ancestors if they could please line up in a row for me. They got into position and jostled each other like a bunch of teenagers before finally putting their arms around each other's shoulders. They smiled widely and looked so youthful. If I'd only had a camera! From left to right were Finity, George, Robert, Keith and Jack.

"Dad, get over there, too," I said, and Dad took his place next to Grandpa Jack.

"That sure is a handsome group of men," Mom said. "Even with that old-timer on the end."

They all kidded Dad, and the image of those wonderful men lined up together will stay with me throughout my life.

They said good-bye and wished me luck, then they vanished one by one. George held back a little, then whispered in my ear, "David North wanted me to tell you how proud he is of you. He knows things worked out for the best, and he's happy you and Tad have found each other."

I wiped away a tear that had suddenly cropped up. "Tell him I feel the same way."

"I will," George said. "We'll see you soon." Then he was gone, leaving only my parents and Grandpa Jack and Grandma Sheila with me at the gravesite.

"We're not quite done here yet," Grandpa Jack said. "Follow me. My mission companion is probably getting a bit antsy to have a healthy body."

Chapter Thirty-Nine

"Grandpa, I thought Grandma was your mission companion," I said, thinking of when they'd served a mission together in upstate New York after Grandpa retired.

"That's true, but I've also been able to serve a mission in the spirit world," he said emotionally. "In fact, I've been serving with Daniel."

Dad seemed startled. "You mean Doug's son?"

Grandma Sheila nodded. "Inside that crippled little body was one of Heavenly Father's most valiant spirits. Daniel's an amazing person."

Grandpa Jack put his arm through mine. "Remember all the temple work you did in the 1990s? Well, most of those people had accepted the gospel in the spirit world, but some still had some questions and difficulties. That's where Daniel came in. He was such a masterful teacher that he converted all the holdouts and then organized them into a missionary force that taught the gospel to thousands more. I did my part, but Daniel was the motivator. In fact, that's why I died so soon after he did. He requested that I be his junior companion!"

Grandpa slowed down and linked his other arm with Grandma Sheila. "Dear, go ahead and tell them what you've been doing on the other side."

Grandma Sheila's eyes lit up. "Remember how I always wanted to be a travel agent or a tour guide? Well, my assignment in Paradise was to greet new arrivals and give them a personalized tour of the spirit world. They were fairly easy to impress, since they'd just come from earth. Each person had their own interests, so the tour was never the same. I loved every moment of it!"

Grandpa turned to me and whispered just loud enough for the others to hear. "She wouldn't tell you this, but she was easily the most popular tour guide. I think it's her dazzling smile."

We reached the graves of Becky and Daniel, and Grandpa explained, "This would normally be Doug's duty, but I've been assigned to fill in for him, since he's still mortal."

Grandpa then called Becky forth from the grave, and she embraced each of us. "Emma, you look wonderful," she said.

"So do you," I said, nearly overwhelmed by her spiritual presence. "I've heard so many good things about you. Thanks for marrying Doug."

She smiled. "I'm glad he was still available after my mission. When you go back, don't let him get married off before I get my head on straight!"

We quieted down as Grandpa called forth Daniel. I had to do a double-take as his body worked its way through the ground. "He's so little," I said as a small child shook out the kinks in his legs and stood up.

"Thank you, Grandpa," Daniel said. Then he leaped into his mother's arms. She hugged him tightly. "Oh, it's fun to see you as a little boy again."

Becky then turned to me and said, "In the spirit world he was a full-grown spirit, of course, and he just didn't feel like my little boy. But now he does, even though he talks like an adult. I can't wait to raise him." She gave him another tight squeeze, then she put him down.

Grandpa put his hand on Daniel's shoulder. "It's great to be taller than you again," he said.

"Don't worry, I'll catch up with you soon enough," Daniel said mischievously.

It was wonderful to see their fully restored bodies, but I had a nagging question. "Becky and Daniel, you both suffered many physical problems when you were mortal," I said. "Do you..."

My question now sounded dumb, but I asked it anyway. "Do you have any regrets or have bad feelings about the suffering you endured?"

They both shook their heads. "That was part of our mission in life," Daniel said.

"The only regret would've been if I'd made spiritual mistakes," Becky said. "One of my sisters committed some serious sins and didn't repent. She's still in the spirit world paying for her actions. She knows she forfeited eternal life in the Celestial Kingdom for shallow, earthly desires. So while my physical setbacks are long-forgotten, my sister's spiritual setbacks still affect her. See what I'm saying?"

"I do. Thank you."

I became aware of a young couple in white robes walking toward us from the older part of the cemetery. I didn't recognize them until the woman said, "You were right, Emma. I *was* attractive when I was younger."

"Leah Jensen?" I nearly shouted as I recognized my neighbor and friend. "You look stunning!"

"I'm Leah Jensen Milton now, thanks to the sealing you and Tad did in our behalf. Please meet my husband, Harold."

Harold stepped forward and greeted us all. He was very handsome and polite, and I could see now why Leah had waited her whole life to be reunited with him.

"How is your sister Beth doing?" I asked.

"She's very happy," Leah said. "She met a man in the spirit world who had died as a missionary at age 19, and they really hit it off. They want to be sealed as soon the temples start running again."

Grandpa stepped forward as Leah said that. "I'm truly sorry to interrupt your reunion, but speaking of temples, we've got a lot to accomplish in a short time. Mark and Michelle, you need to return to the Provo Temple and get it fully operational. With nearly all of the temples having been closed for a few years, there's quite a backlog of righteous spirits waiting to have their work done. So schedule your workers in three 8-hour shifts each day so the temple can operate continuously."

Grandpa turned to Leah. "I'm glad you mentioned Beth and her newfound love. I crossed paths with them not long ago in the spirit world and she made me promise to put her at the top of the Provo Temple's sealing list. So I'll get you that information as soon as I can, Mark."

Grandpa then turned to Becky and Daniel. "You two will now go to New Jerusalem and reacquaint yourselves with your families. Also, tell Doug and Tad to bring everyone back here—including his whole ward. We'll need them to staff the temple and perform the ordinances."

Finally Grandpa Jack turned to face me. "How are you feeling, granddaughter?"

"Wonderful," I said. "I'm eager to help in any way I can."

"You will be a great help," Grandpa said. "Be a strong example for the rest of us."

"What are you saying?"

"The time has come for you to return to the past. Besides, we need your 'older self' to return and help Tad get things organized. See you soon."

"No, don't say that," I pleaded. "I don't want to go back!"

Before I could even react, Grandpa kissed me lightly on the forehead, and everything began to fade away. I caught a glimpse of little Daniel's smiling face as I stumbled backward. Then I was gone.

Chapter Forty

A frigid breeze chilled me to the bone, and I found myself in a swirling snowstorm. I moved under a pine tree for shelter, and I realized I was still in the Evergreen Cemetery, but it certainly was no longer during the Millennium. Cars were passing by on the road south of the cemetery and two men were using a backhoe and a dumptruck to dig a grave about 50 yards away, not far from Grandpa Keith's headstone.

I looked across the valley at barren, snow-covered West Mountain. Gray clouds shrouded its top. To the north I could see the Kimball Tower rising above the BYU campus. Everything seemed just as it should on a typical winter day in Utah County.

I found myself staring at a headstone with a cute little lamb carved into its top, and I realized it was the same headstone I'd admired following Leah's funeral. I was getting really confused. Had these errands all just been a dream?

Then I looked at my clothing. I was wearing a beautiful light-colored dress—the same one I'd worn to Brother Newman's funeral. I knew I'd worn a blue denim jumper to Leah's funeral, and I smiled to know it hadn't been a dream! Besides, it had been dreadfully hot that day, and now I was shivering to death. But how ironic to end my journey at the spot where I'd started my adventures.

I was standing on an area where no one had been buried yet, and I realized it was where Becky and Daniel would someday be laid to rest. As I thought of them, I could almost feel the lingering effects of that glorious future day when they'd rise from the grave. I raised my eyebrows and could still feel where Grandpa Jack's immortal lips had rested on my forehead, and suddenly I felt very depressed.

"No! Let me be with them!" I shouted at the sky. I'd seen so many glorious things, and I couldn't imagine just going home and resuming normal life again. My emotions broke loose, and I began weeping.

The sound of the nearby backhoe had nearly drowned out the arrival of a blue Nissan, which had turned onto the small paved road to the west of me. I looked up as the driver waved and then got out of the car. My tears changed to laughter as a tall man with dark hair and whiskers walked toward me. He wore a cloak and sandals.

I jumped to my feet and ran to him. "Mathoni! What a welcome sight you are!"

Mathoni gave me a strange stare, unsure how to react. But he stood his ground, and I fell into his arms. "Oh, you're just who I wanted to see," I said.

He held me gently for a moment before asking, "How do you know my name?"

"I know everything about you," I said. "How did you know where to find me?"

Those marvelous blue eyes studied my face for a long time. In 2,000 years he'd surely never encountered this predicament. "I was guided here," he finally answered. "You seem fine, though. Do you need assistance?"

"Can you give me a ride home?" I asked, suddenly feeling much better. "I'll explain how I know you on the way to my parents' house."

We walked through the blizzard to the car, and I waved happily to the elderly gentleman standing near the backhoe. The man seemed very curious about Mathoni's cloak, and he pointed us out to the younger man operating the backhoe. They both watched us intently as we approached the car. Finally the young man just smiled and shrugged, while the older man waved back and pleasantly shouted, "Get out of the storm, you crazy kids! You'll freeze to death!"

I waved again to the men, then joined Mathoni in the car. "Of course, you could never freeze to death, could you, Mathoni?"

"How do you know that?" he asked warily as we exited the cemetery and turned onto 400 East.

"Like I said, I know all about you. Thanks for wearing the cloak. It helped me identify you more easily." Mathoni was now fuming a little, and I realized I needed to ease his mind.

"I apologize for teasing you," I said. "I've got a glorious story to tell you, and maybe I should share it with you before you take me home. Why don't we take a ride through the fields and out to West Mountain? That should give me enough time to fill you in on how I know you."

He glanced at me sideways. "Whatever you say, Emma."

• • • •

An hour later when Mathoni parked his car in the driveway behind Doug's Volkswagen, we were chatting just like old...well, future friends. "Would you like to come in and meet my family?" I asked.

Mathoni shook his head. "I feel something's brewing in Ogden," he said. "I need to get up there before sunset. But thanks for telling me about your latest errand, and I'm glad I could help. I mean I'm glad I *will* help."

"You're wonderful," I said. "I'll probably see you in a few decades!"

He smiled and shook my hand. "Stay strong, Emma. Every faithful Saint makes a big difference in this world."

"I'll do my best. Take care."

I watched him drive away, then I hurried to the front door, entered the living room, and called out, "Has anyone been missing a daughter or sister?"

I heard my parents' surprised cries from the kitchen, and Doug's bedroom door flew open. He spotted me and soon gripped me in a tight hug. Mom and Dad joined us within seconds, and we all embraced silently for nearly a minute.

Finally we broke apart, and Mom looked at me carefully. "You look absolutely radiant, Emma. I'm so happy you're back."

"Did you go into the future?" Doug asked excitedly.

"I did! And I must congratulate you on figuring out where I was," I said. "I read your book while I was there. You did a great job."

"Really?" Doug asked. "That seems weird, since it won't be in stores until next week! But I'm glad you liked it."

"It was wonderful."

"So was this a leisurely errand?" Dad asked. "Just lying around reading books?"

I laughed and shook my head. "No, this was a fantastic errand. And you each play a role in preparing the church for the Second Coming."

They seemed shocked. "We do?" Doug asked. "We're just the Daltons."

"Great things await each of you," I said. "I'm eager to tell you about it, but let Tad get here first. I can't wait to wrap my arms around his young, well-toned body."

The others laughed. "I'm guessing none of us keep our youthful figures in future years," Doug said thoughtfully.

"Actually, you hold up the best, Doug," I said.

I picked up the phone and called Tad, who shouted for joy to hear my voice. He said he'd be there as quickly as possible.

• • • •

I returned to the living room and saw Doug talking on the porch to a blonde woman in her early 20s. He even nuzzled her ear a little.

"Who's that?" I asked Mom.

"That's Blair Hansen," she said happily. "She and Doug are getting pretty serious, and I wouldn't be surprised if they get engaged soon."

"Engaged?"

"Yes, she's a wonderful girl," Mom said.

I shook my head. "I'm sure she's nice, but she's not the one for Doug."

Mom's head pivoted around. "you'd better not jinx this, Emma, especially after all the heartache he had with Becky."

"I'll stay out of it, but just trust me," I said.

Doug noticed I was off the phone, and he brought Blair into the house to introduce me. I was very polite, but I knew in my heart this woman would never be my sister-in-law. I just couldn't picture Doug without Becky—or without Justin, Heather and Daniel. Those three kids had tenacity, and I was sure they were doing everything in their power on the other side of the veil to get Becky and Doug together. Against those three, Blair didn't have a chance. Of course, I'd do all I could, too.

Blair had just stopped by on her way to work. She soon left, and Doug sauntered back into the room. "What do you think of her, Emma?"

"She's cute and seems very pleasant," I said as enthusiastically as possible.

Doug glanced at our parents, then peered into my eyes. "You don't like her," he said dejectedly. "Why not?"

I shrugged and asked, "What about Becky Brown?"

Doug's eyes bulged out. "How do you even know about her?"

"Don't forget, I read your book while in the future."

Doug bristled. "Well, things didn't work out between Becky and me, and I'm sorry I even mentioned her in the book."

"Fine," I said calmly. "But I can't imagine anyone else as my sister-in-law."

I had touched a tender nerve. Doug breathed deeply and began pacing, but a glimmer of hope filled his eyes. "What did you see in that future world? Is there still a chance between me and Becky?"

Dad interrupted. "Emma, you don't realize what Becky has put Doug through! She plays mind games and seems very unsettled."

I scoffed. "She's still young and unsure of herself. Give her some time to get her head on straight."

"Let's just drop the subject," Doug said. "Becky is very serious with a BYU basketball player named Chris Taggart. I even got in a fist fight with Chris over her and he broke his hand, which made me quite unpopular in this valley. Besides, once Chris joins the NBA, they'll probably get married."

I rolled my eyes and said, "Don't worry about that Taggart kid. He's not NBA material. Here's the real question: Does Blair make your heart thump like Becky does?"

He shifted his feet. "Well, no."

I smiled. "Then things will work out. After all, it's because of your children—and Becky's—that I was sent into the future."

Doug was speechless, yet grinning from ear to ear.

"Just let Blair down softly," I said.

Doug gave me an uncertain look. "Did you happen to meet Becky while you were in the future?" he asked.

"I sure did. Believe me, she's worth the wait."

Chapter Forty-One

I ran outside to meet Tad as he pulled into the driveway. He looked so handsome, and I clung tightly to him after giving him a long kiss. I also couldn't keep my hands out of his hair. "I love you so much," I whispered. "Let's not stay here too long. We've got to get started on our family."

Tad blushed but mumbled, "Hey, whatever you say."

We returned to the house, and I filled them in on what I'd experienced. They listened eagerly, somewhat surprised at the changes that will take place in the world.

"I'm so excited these things will happen in our lifetime," Tad said. "It won't be easy, but we'll be part of some amazing events."

Dad had listened intently, but he hadn't said much. I finally asked, "Dad, what's on your mind?"

"I'm just wondering how much of what you experienced *must* come true," he said. "We obviously have no control over the earthquakes and the wars and the floods, and certainly we wouldn't want to alter the establishment of Zion. I'm also pleased with the outcome for our family, but maybe there's a way to avoid some of the unpleasantness you saw."

"Are you talking about the Salt Lake Gladiatorzz?" Doug asked slyly.

"Well, I certainly hope we help avoid that team ever being formed," Dad said with a laugh. "But I'm just saying that what Emma experienced isn't set in stone, since those events haven't happened yet. The Lord often makes conditional prophecies of destruction that can be avoided if we repent or change our behavior. Maybe part of the purpose of Emma's experience was to show us ways to improve before the future actually gets here."

"What areas do you have in mind, honey?" Mom asked.

"For example, Emma's dangerous journey to Lincoln Point. It sounds like it could've been avoided if I'd just watched Justin a little better," Dad said. "Or maybe we'll have to send Becky and the kids to New Jerusalem. We'll just have to stay on our toes."

. . . .

Dad's words about altering the future stayed in my mind, and about a week later I returned to Springville to see Angie Newman's parents. I knocked on the door, and Brother Newman greeted me. "Hello, Emma. I haven't seen you in a while. Come on in."

Thank you, Brother Newman," I said. "You look so young...and alive."

"Thanks for the compliment," he chortled. "Flora, come in here. We've got a guest—a very kind guest, I might add."

Sister Newman came in and gave me a surprised hug. We exchanged some small talk, then I asked them how Angie was doing.

"She's been through a lot of ups and downs. Well, mostly downs," Brother Newman said. "Right now she's living in an apartment on the west side of town with her little boy. She's trying to make it on her own, but she moves back in with us when she runs out of money. She just seems lost."

"The baby's father isn't around?" I asked.

"He left town once Angie told him she was pregnant," Sister Newman said. "We aren't too sad. He was a wild kid who was always getting into trouble."

"I'm so sorry to hear that," I said. "I haven't talked with Angie since the summer after high school, and I feel I need to see her."

Sister Newman nodded. "That would be wonderful," she said. "I don't want to hurt your feelings, but Angie feels you abandoned her. She knows she slipped off the right path, and I'm afraid she resents you now for staying strong in the church."

Brother Newman reached across the sofa and touched my knee. "But talking with you would do her a lot of good," he said. "Just smile if she spouts a little venom."

"I think I can handle it," I said. "I just want to be her friend again."

. . . .

I followed their directions to Angie's apartment. It was on

the bottom floor of a run-down four-plex, and I could hear the sound of a TV as I approached.

I rang the doorbell and worriedly waited, unable to get Serena the High Priestess out of my mind. But the girl who opened the door was my friend Angie, just a little heavier with dark bags under her eyes.

"Hmmpt," she said in surprise. "What brings you here? This isn't exactly your part of town."

"I just thought I'd stop by and say hello," I said with a nervous smile. "We have a lot of catching up to do."

Angie cocked her head and gave me that arrogant look she'd mastered. "I'm a little busy right now. Maybe some other time."

No, I've waited long enough already to visit you," I said. "Just give me five minutes."

Angie stared at the ground for several seconds. "Ah, whatever," she finally said. "Come on in. Please ignore the mess."

She walked over to the TV and turned off a soap opera, then moved a pile of clothes she'd been folding to the edge of the couch. "Take a seat," she said. "Would you like a soda?"

"Sure," I said as I sat next to the pile of clothes. My eyes were drawn to a pair of little boy overalls. I picked them up and folded them in half, then gently touched the little basketball embroidered on the front.

"You don't have to fold those," Angie said as she returned with our drinks.

"Oh, I was just feeling a little envious of you," I said.

Angie looked shocked. "Why?"

"Well, Tad and I have been trying to have a child, but we haven't had any luck."

"I wish I'd had that problem," Angie said with a sad chuckle.

"Anyway, you've already got a little boy, and you're making it on your own," I said. "I'm proud of you."

Angie frowned. "You have no reason to be proud of me. I've said some pretty rude things about you the past few years."

I shrugged. "I've probably deserved whatever you said. I haven't exactly been a good friend to you."

Angie stared out the window. "I guess I've blamed you for the trouble I've gotten into, but I know it was my own fault for chasing after the wrong crowd. You got married in the temple, and Brandee cleaned herself up and went to Snow College, but I got pregnant and became a single mom. I just felt like my friends thought they were better than me, and deep down I knew it was true."

"Don't say that," I pleaded. "You're an awesome girl! You've got your whole life ahead of you! You know what? My brother Doug was even wondering if you'd like to go out on a double-date with Tad and me."

The words were out before I'd even realized it. Doug would make me pay dearly, but it would be worth it if I could change Angie's course in life.

Angie's eyes showed some life for the first time. "Doug would actually go on a date with me?"

"Well, you know, you'd go just as friends," I said hastily. "I think we'd have a fun time. Maybe we could go bowling or out to eat."

Angie nodded. "I'd been planning to try out a new Salt Lake nightclub this weekend, but I haven't been on a real date since Nick split town. Let's do it!"

A cry reached us from the back bedroom. "It sounds like Thomas is awake. Would you like to meet him?"

"Certainly." I followed Angie back to the bedroom, where a husky little boy with flaming red hair was pulling himself out of the crib! "He's strong," I said. "How old is he?"

"He just turned eleven months old," Angie said. "But he'll climb anything and sometimes even flips himself out of the crib. I call him 'Mighty Tom' when he does that."

The nickname triggered a flashback. I looked at Tom's red hair and peered into his mischievous eyes, and I couldn't help stumbling backward as a realization hit me.

This infant was The Mighty One!

"Are you all right?" Angie asked worriedly.

"Uh, yeah. Just feeling a little dizzy," I said. "Can we go back to the couch?"

When we were settled again Tom climbed up my legs and sat on my lap. "He really seems to like you," Angie said. "He usually doesn't let strangers hold him."

I ruffled his red hair and he smiled—just before he threw up all over me. "I'm so sorry," Angie said as she jumped to her feet.

"Let me grab a wet towel."

When Angie left the room I cupped Tom's little cheeks in my hands and whispered, "I'm keeping my eye on you for the rest of your life, bucko. If I see you even throw a water balloon, I'm calling the cops." Then I put him on the floor and started to clean myself up.

Angie returned and said, "Well, I hope you and Tad have a child soon. Maybe Tom and your child could become friends." I thought of my future son Dave and felt he'd be up to the task, even though the boys would be a couple of years apart.

"That sounds good," I said sincerely. "I'd like that."

So maybe there's a chance Mighty Tom will excel in something other than post-World War III looting raids.

Chapter Forty-Two

As I type these final words, I'm six months pregnant with our first child. To Tad's delight, the ultrasound showed we are definitely having a boy. We've decided to name him David, but I have a feeling he'll prefer being called Dave.

Doug was a good sport about going out with Angie. We double-dated a few times and he even took her to church twice. Then one night Angie called him and asked if he'd mind if she started dating someone else. She'd met a returned missionary at her job, and things were looking good between them. She said the guy even adored baby Tom!

I called her as soon as Doug told me the news. "Congratulations, Angie! I'm so excited for you," I said. "I'm eager to meet him. What's his name?"

"Kyle Thomason," she said. "He grew up in Wyoming but has moved down here. He treats me so kindly."

I happily pumped my fist in the air. Any name other than Larry "Sherem" Campbell was wonderful. Angie told me Kyle accepted her wholeheartedly despite her past mistakes, and she sounded very happy for the first time in years.

It's still early in Angie's reformation, but I'm confident I'll never again cross paths with Serena the High Priestess. I also feel sure that Steve Young's uniform won't ever be worn by a red-haired tribal chieftain.

Meanwhile, Doug is keeping in touch with Becky, who's more than halfway done with her mission in the Canary Islands. He also showed me a newspaper article last week that said Chris Taggart is playing well in France, so things are falling into place. I hope Chris has a long career overseas.

• • • •

So while my time-travel errands are over, I feel my mission in life has only begun. I've witnessed the wonderful things that await the righteous people of the earth, but now comes the hard part—getting back to where I once was. I've already got a list of things to do, such as keep an eye on Tom, get to know Tara's parents, somehow locate Devri in a few years, etc.

However, my journey into the future has given me great hope. I don't fear the natural disasters or even the wars that will certainly come. I only fear not following the Lord and His prophets. Each day I strive to become the type of person who might again meet the Savior of the World. Any sacrifice is worth being in His presence again.

And the wonderful thing is that you—yes, you—will also be playing a role in this incredible journey into the future. So say hello if we cross paths, and don't forget to bring along your friends and family.

We're going to have a great time!

About the Author

Chad G. Daybell lives in Springville, Utah, with his wife, Tammy, and their five children. He graduated from BYU with a bachelor's degree in Journalism, where he served as the city editor of *The Daily Universe*.

Following graduation he worked for three years as a copy editor at *The Standard-Examiner* in Ogden, Utah, before returning to his home town to serve as Springville's cemetery sexton. It was during his time as sexton that he wrote the Emma Trilogy. After four years in that unique profession, he accepted employment as the manager of a computer supply company in Provo.

Chad served an LDS mission among the Spanish-speaking people of New Jersey, and he has served in several capacities in the church. He enjoys spending time with his wife and children, following the local sports teams and working in his yard.

Chad welcomes your comments at his internet website **www.cdaybell.com** where you can ask him questions about the Emma Trilogy and read about the true stories that inspired it.

The website also has a collection of the specific prophecies Chad used to shape *Escape to Zion*.

So stop in at the site and say hello!